SINCERITY

SINCERITY

THE RECIPE FOR LIVING
YOUR BEST PERSONAL AND
PROFESSIONAL LIFE

AARON BROOKS

NEW DEGREE PRESS

SINCERITY

The Recipe for Living Your Best Personal and Professional Life

ISBN   978-1-63676-700-0 *Paperback*
          978-1-63730-067-1 *Kindle Ebook*
          978-1-63730-169-2 *Ebook*

This book is dedicated to the most important people in my life—my family. My wife Lisa is my best friend and has always been my biggest cheerleader, and I simply could not have done this without her. My three kids, Andrew, Dylan, and Leo, who inspire me in everything I do. And, of course, my Golden Retrievers, Jerry and Scarlet, who make me smile every single day

Contents

—

Introduction

———

Loren Michaels Harris dumped a bag of about a hundred business cards out on the table in front of me.

I was introduced to Loren through someone else I had met who felt Loren and I should know one another, and Loren had asked to interview me about my book for his online show. It was during that conversation he excitedly pulled out this bag of cards.

Sincere relationships with other human beings are not only extremely important to Loren personally, but they are vital to his long-term professional success. He is a motivational speaker, TV host, and entertainer who runs his own web-based TV show for which he personally needs to identify five interesting and insightful guests per week.

Loren lived in twenty-two foster homes as a child and has a unique gift of sharing his story with others, significantly motivating them when doing so. In order to identify groups to speak to and guests for his shows, Loren knows relationships are vital.

Growing up, Loren needed to adapt to new environments and get to know new people quickly, so he developed a natural ability to let people in and build sincere relationships. In many ways, this skill was vital to his survival. For Loren, this has always been very clear, and I am here to tell you the ability to build and foster sincere relationships may be more important to your overall happiness and success than you might think.

"These business cards all represent someone who has reached out to me and given me their card, or someone I met at a networking or other such event. I don't even remember most of them, and I only actually know about ten of them," Loren shared. When I asked Loren what was different about these ten relationships, he said "sincerity" without missing a beat.

Like many to whom I refer to in this book, Loren has met most of the people he is close to through other friends and connections. Some people who you will meet at networking and other events will be genuine and sincere, and a deeper relationship will emerge; but more people approach these events transactionally, and these transactional behaviors do not create the beginnings of the best possible relationships.

Most people clearly are trying to play the numbers game, and most people are not sincerely interested in building a real relationship. Rather, when most people say they are interested in building a relationship, they are really looking for a shortcut to taking as much out of a relationship as possible while putting the least amount of work into it. Unfortunately, this is the way people have been taught to do business, and this transactional approach does not lend itself to building sincere relationships.

In this book, we will discuss relationship building and most importantly, we will discuss how to do this important activity in a way where it helps others while still helping yourself—in a way that really feels good.

This is something I have done a lot of over the past thirty years of my career and life. I have spent the majority of my career in business development roles for professional services firms such as consulting, accounting, staffing, and now digital marketing.

Over the years, many people seem to realize networking is truly important. At the same time, most people do not really know how to "network," and only do so when they are looking for a job or a new client. Many of the people we really want to get to know have virtually no interest in networking. Therefore, a new definition of networking is needed.

Those who have built the sincerest and most valuable professional networks build, maintain, and foster relationships with a sincere approach that simply cannot be faked. They constantly meet new people, look for ways to give selflessly, and are disciplined in ensuring their approach to building these new relationships. These are the people who I have found to be the most fulfilled and successful.

I have had the same conversation about networking and sincere relationships what seems like hundreds of times throughout my career and my life. People will always have you believe their intent is sincere—but as they say, "The proof is in the pudding."

The word "networking" is overused and under-defined. When asked if they have the time to network, most senior executives feel they are simply too busy to network based on their perception of what networking is. Since most people don't really know how to network effectively, they come into networking conversations with their hand out, asking for favors with little to offer to the other side. Therefore, the activity of networking has become commoditized, and is of little value to many people.

The people with whom you *really* want to network know the difference between those who are looking to build a sincere relationship and someone who is just looking for a handout. I have found using the frameworks described later in this book will allow you to build relationships with those you want to know, which will allow you to find the highest levels of fulfillment and success. But first, let's discuss...

WHAT DOES "NETWORKING" REALLY MEAN?

Often, when people think of the word "networking," they think of attending large events, collecting business cards, and trying to figure out after that how to engage with other attendees to create a *transaction* or some sort of short-term goal, be it a job or a business deal (trying to sell something).

If we learned anything during the COVID-19 pandemic in 2020 and 2021, it was we cannot rely on the ability to attend in-person events where we meet new people with whom to do business. We need to be more intentional in our approach to relationships.

In March 2020, life changed overnight—literally. People were forced to stay inside and do business through a screen. No one could go into offices, and we could not see our friends, families, and business associates in person. Deep relationships became even more important, and those who had maintained them were able to thrive.

According to a recent LinkedIn global survey, almost 80 percent of professionals consider business networking to be important to career success. Additionally, 70 percent of people in 2016 were hired at a company where they had a connection.[1]

Despite these overwhelming statistics, networking attitudes do not match behaviors.

Thirty-eight percent of those globally surveyed said they find it hard to stay in touch with their network. This network typically consists of former clients, coworkers, and others who have somehow touched their lives professionally. Nearly half (49 percent) globally said this is because they do not have the time. Perhaps even more interesting is despite the fact the majority (79 percent) globally agrees professional networking is valuable for career progression, less than half (48 percent) globally say they keep in touch with their network when things are going well in their career. [2]

Given that many people agree networking is important and valuable, people are not engaging in this activity as much as

---

1   "Eighty-Percent of Professionals Consider Networking Important to Career Success," LinkedIn Corporate Communications, LinkedIn Pressroom, June 22, 2017.

2   Ibid.

they seem to realize they should. My experience tells me this is often because they do not know how to.

A NEW DEFINITION OF NETWORKING

Those who approach networking solely from a transactional point of view are not the most successful. Like a brand that consistently represents itself in the marketplace, people need to ensure they are consistently meeting others so people are aware of them when opportunities arise.

As consumers, we cannot buy a product we do not know about, and the philosophies and processes discussed in this book will help the reader ensure they are amongst those people who develop real, sincere, organic relationships and enjoy the long-term success that goes along with this. It's no surprise these individuals tend to live the most fulfilled lives.

Later in the book, you will read about Benny Mathew, a young professional in Chicago who built a tremendous network completely on his own. This network compliments and enables his professional life. Many of those in his network are people with whom he does business; however, this is *never* forced. Everything about Benny is genuine. His energy is infectious, and he is enjoying tremendous personal and professional success largely as a result of this approach.

"I look at relationships as a way to get to know and understand people's real goals, with no goal other than to sincerely get to know them. I am never sure where that might lead, but I am always open to the possibilities."

Those who develop authentic, sincere relationships and friendships enter every new relationship looking to provide any assistance they can while expecting very little to nothing out of those they meet. People of this caliber will act with a sincerity that cannot be faked. This will be a consistent theme in the stories told throughout this book.

You cannot fake sincerity. When people are sincere, you know it. When people are insincere, you know this as well.

There are many ways of creating sincere value in a new relationship, and those who live this life create value first through listening—really listening. They seek to understand the goals of those they get to know, holistically. Most of us want to talk about ourselves and are thinking about what we want to accomplish, but we need to defer to others and listen to understand what they are truly passionate about. If we can help them accomplish these things over time, our relationships will deepen.

"Listening is intrinsic to human relationships. Done well, it's a powerful talent, and when freely given, a momentous gift."

LLOYD MINOR, MD, CARL AND ELIZABETH
NAUMANN DEAN OF THE SCHOOL OF
MEDICINE, STANFORD UNIVERSITY [3]

When most people are introduced to someone new, it is for a specific reason, like a client who needs some type of

---

3   Lloyd Minor, "Listening is Fundamental: The mystery of sound and how it affects us," *Stanford Medicine*, Spring 2018.

service, for instance. The person who is trying to *close a deal* is usually fixated on closing the business and successfully providing the service. However, while this success might have a positive impact on that company's bottom line, they usually don't even think about how this success does or does not impact that particular person. If we approach these new relationships through a 360-degree, multi-dimensional lens, seeking to understand the personal goals of these people rather than only focusing on the goals of their company we can completely change the entire dynamic of the relationships. This happens quickly.

One of the best gifts we can give when we meet someone is an introduction to another person who can help them now or in the future. After all, companies do not make hiring decisions, or decide from whom to purchase products and services; people make these decisions.

THE BEST TIME TO MEET PEOPLE IS BEFORE YOU NEED TO KNOW THEM

Furthermore, as we meet new people, if we help them understand why this proactive approach to relationships is so important, the dynamics of our relationships with these people in the future will change as well. They will create relationships for us, and these relationships will lead to opportunities over time, since trust is already present. If we become evangelists for new relationships, it becomes inspiring and infectious to those around us.

One thing I have heard over and over in the world of sales is, people do business or buy from people they *like*. However, in my experience, it goes deeper than that; people will buy from people they *trust,* and trust is earned. For instance, those who represent professional services such as consulting firms, accounting, and law firms count on the personal relationships they have built with people in the marketplace to allow them to close the largest deals. These sincere relationships have only become more important.

Unfortunately, business has become less personal over the past fifteen years, especially since so many businesses operate online. Prior to the proliferation of the internet, if we were looking for insurance for our family or a new banking relationship, we had to deal with other human beings. Today, we are able to simply pull out our laptop, and with a few keystrokes, we can accomplish these things without ever talking with another person.

These same dynamics are at play for companies, and this has created a situation where company leaders are building fewer organic relationships than in the past.

CHAPTER 1

The Future of Relationships

———

We are at a point in history where sincere relationships are not only important, but they are also becoming vital for personal and professional success.

Prior to the internet, if a partner in a CPA firm, for example, wanted to reach the CEO or CFO of a company to pitch an idea, they would simply pick up the phone and the call would be answered! If it was not answered by that leader, it would have been answered by a human being who would convey the message and ensure it was returned. In other words, if you were attempting to get to know these types of people from a business or personal perspective, they were open to taking a call.

When I left Accenture and joined Robert Half International, they handed me a list of companies and asked me to cold-call the executives in these companies to sell them services. This was in 2003, and some executives were still answering their own calls. One of those executives was Janet Zelenka, VP of Internal Audit at a company called United Stationers. After cold-calling her and doing the pitch they taught me, she invited me in to see her. In 2003, all public companies needed to comply with the new Sarbanes-Oxley Act that had come out of the recent accounting scandals with Enron and other companies, and companies such as United Stationers needed to comply with this new law. Doing so required resources most of these companies did not have, therefore requiring them to bring in additional, temporary accounting staff, and these were the services I represented.

While we had a great first meeting, we did not end up doing business together. We stayed in touch over the years, getting together regularly to discuss family and business. Today, Janet is CFO/CIO of another public company, and over the years, we have built a trusting relationship and friendship that truly transcends business.

A few years ago, after joining a new firm, I asked Janet why she was always willing to meet with me whenever I joined a new firm. Her answer was very interesting, telling, and was something like, "Aaron, first of all, you never come across like you are trying to sell anything. You come across like you are sincerely looking to add value, bring a new approach, or help someone personally." This conversation took place in approximately 2013, but I remember it like it was yesterday. After that, I got to know Janet's son Michael, and he subsequently did an internship with my firm.

It is truly amazing what happens when sincere relationships develop.

Today, the dynamics of *selling* services have changed drastically. Executives do not answer their own calls, and rather than having a human assistant, they often have electronic means of answering and screening your call. My experience has told me it is very difficult to be successful in sales using solely a cold-calling approach. A sincere relationship approach is really the only way for long-term success.

According to Vocabulary.com, sincerity is defined as "the quality of being open and truthful; not deceitful or hypocritical."[4] This definition certainly makes sense. We all want to deal with people who we feel are sincere; if we feel they are sincere and kind, we will trust them. At the end of the day, sincerity is a feeling that is difficult to put your finger on, but when it is there, you know it.

To me, sincerity is simply defined as a relationship with another person in which you truly and authentically want to help them as if they were your closest friend. While I am not holier-than-thou, my definition of sincerity is being happy to do something for another person with *no expectation of something in return,* and my network knows this because I live this life every single day. I have not only told them, but I have also proven it with the consistent behaviors I outline throughout this book. This is where the rubber meets the road.

There is a very easy question you can ask others, and when answered, follow up with any promises made. "What can I do to help you?" If we ask this question through a professional

---

4   *Vocabulary Online,* s.v. "Sincerity," accessed February 14, 2021.

and a personal lens, it is amazing what happens. You may find out someone's child is trying to get an internship with a company in which you know someone, and if this happens, I suggest making an introduction. These types of gestures go incredibly far in building the long-term, sincere relationships to which I refer throughout this book.

Most of the sales managers and staffing, CPA, or consulting firm partners I worked with over the years think they have a very strong understanding of what quality, mutually beneficial relationships truly are in today's business climate. At the end of the day, the bar on what constitutes a mutually beneficial relationship has been raised, and people need to deeply consider how these dynamics have changed over the years. This shift is because of the impersonal approach of internet-based and technology-enabled selling, as well as the fact people rarely answer their own phones, and leaders like my friend Janet Zelenka simply do not have the time to be "sold to." Once these leaders trust you as a person, they are more than willing to take your calls, listen to your ideas, and possibly do business with you and your firm.

Growing up, I watched my father build a bakery supply manufacturing and distributing business. He and his partners literally built a business from the ground up, almost solely through the power of building sincere, trusting relationships in which they treated people as they would like to be treated. As I moved from working in my father's business to working in the professional world, I found most, if not all, of the most successful and fulfilled people were those who built and maintained sincere relationships that endured the test of time. I benefited substantially from these types of relationships and have helped others build these types of relationships themselves, something that helped me build even better relationships with these people. These are the people I discuss throughout this book.

Many people think what matters most is how many people you know or have in your personal network. However, to be most successful, you must become a *sincere connector*.

SINCERE CONNECTORS

It does not really matter how many people you know. It matters more how many people know one another *as a result of your efforts*, how many connections you create for others, and staying consistent in these behaviors.

Most people think of "networking" as something they do when they need to make something happen now, rather than as a way of life. For some people, this will be really easy, for some, this might be difficult. In my experience, the key to unlocking your best, most profound and consistent life is to live a life of *sincerity* in everything you do.

This book will explore and help you understand why the most effective currency one can accumulate today is not money; rather, it is the sincere relationships we build, the people we look to authentically help throughout the journeys of our personal and professional lives, and the relationships we are given in return.

Every single day, the world is changing. These changes are impacting everything about our lives, such as the ways we work, buy and sell products, and build and manage relationships in business and in our lives generally.

For those at the beginning of their career and seeking a road map for how to live their lives and run their careers in a way where they will build relationships now that can benefit them both today and long into the future—this book will help you lay out a personal road map for how you can do this from a relationship perspective.

For those in the middle of their careers and lives, who are looking for ways to develop deeper and more meaningful relationships with those they work with and meet along the way, this book will provide you with a specific philosophy and framework that you can use today and into the future to further differentiate yourself throughout the rest of your career. It will give you the tools you will need to develop the relationships in the marketplace that will allow you to maximize your potential.

For those who are approaching the end of their career, who might like one more professional role but have not nurtured professional relationships in the same way they have their personal ones, this book will give you specific ideas on how you can leverage past business and personal relationships in unique ways that will open up doors that might not have opened in the past.

I will also introduce the concepts of "the 360-degree relationship" and "multi-dimensional relationships." Most of the relationships we develop in our lives have a 180-degree nature, or single dimension to them, meaning we only turn to those relationships when we need something, but rarely, if ever, look to sincerely give into these relationships. Those who are most successful and fulfilled throughout their lives learn to develop 360-degree, multi-dimensional relationships with the stakeholders in their lives, whether they start as friends, business associates, or employees. The relationship I described with Janet above is a perfect example of such a relationship. The 360-degree, multi-dimensional relationship philosophy is one that is completely mutually beneficial, both in philosophy and practice.

This book will explore my personal story and the personal stories of people who have made a substantial difference in the lives of others throughout their lives and careers. Through understanding their stories, along with some specific, concrete ideas you can implement now, this is a book that will help you find the "sincerity" in your life we all so desperately desire and need more and more of, given the world we live in today.

There are lessons to learn from the study of human psychology related to the need for connection to other human beings. In many ways, people are starving for more deep human relationships. According to *Psychology Today*:

- More Americans live alone than ever before.
- One in four Americans report not having a single person to talk to about important issues.
- Loneliness among American adults has increased by 16 percent in the last decade. [5]

5   Kory Floyd, PhD, "What Lack of Affection Can Do to You," *Psychology Today*, August 31, 2013.

According to Northwestern Medicine, the impacts of creating great relationships have been proven to have substantial health benefits related to reduced stress, both at work and at home. These include:

- Less Stress
- Better Healing
- Healthier Behaviors
- Greater Sense of Purpose
- Longer Life[6] (3)

Being around my father for literally my entire life and seeing his example are what truly set the wheels in motion for the way I have approached relationships in my life. When I would go to work with my father as a kid, it meant seeing his customers, who were invariably also friends. I would go to their kids' birthday parties on the weekends and I knew all of them. My father did not do "work-life balance." It was more of a "work-life integration" and to this day, my father still enjoys the same relationships with these people, both personally and professionally.

In March 2020, COVID-19 forced us all into a seclusion the likes of which we have never seen in our lifetimes. As human beings, we crave relationships with other people, and these relationships were cut off. The environment we lived in before COVID-19 was already one where we would benefit substantially through authentic relationships, but COVID made it that much more difficult to create these relationships. This only made living a life where we look to create intentional

---

6   "Five Benefits of Healthy Relationships," Northwestern Medicine, Accessed February 11, 2021.

360-degree, multi-dimensional relationships that much more important. These relationships will leave you much more fulfilled and arm you with relationships that will not only enrich you for the rest of your life, but will better insulate you to weather things outside of your control. The circumstances of COVID-19 made the central message of this book that much more important, which is there is no time like now to develop and maintain the sincere relationships described in this book!

After reading, you will be equipped with the philosophies of living a sincere life, learn about the stories of people who have lived such a life, and be prepared to take the steps yourself to develop these types of amazing relationships which will enable you to enjoy many great things that will happen in your life as a result.

CHAPTER 2

The 360-Degree, Multi-Dimensional Relationship

The phone rang, and I answered. It was late in the evening and the house was getting quiet after we walked the dog. At that time, there were only a few channels on TV, and I would typically watch the local 10:00 p.m. news or *M*A*S*H*. The voice on the other end of the phone was one I recognized, as it was a customer and friend of my father for many years. These late-night calls happened often in our house, and my father always took them. I was probably thirteen at the time.

As I mentioned earlier, my father owned, and still owns, a bakery supply manufacturing and distributing company. I could hear my father's side of the conversation. "Sure. I can jump in the car now, head to my warehouse, and be at your bakery within the next hour or so." He then hung up the phone and went upstairs to get dressed. Given that we lived in the Chicago area, it was often quite cold when these calls would come in. However, that didn't matter. If one his customers needed something, my father would brave the elements to take care of it.

This was one of his clients who had run out of a particular product they needed for the evening's baking, and without it, they could not do a large part of the production for the evening. My father did not even think twice about taking care of this due to the fact his relationships always went beyond just the vendor/customer relationships. He braved the elements, jumped into his car in the north suburbs of Chicago, headed to his warehouse in the city at least forty minutes away, picked up what the customer needed, and personally delivered it. He arrived home after 1:00 a.m. and needed to be up for work by 4:30 a.m.

These were the behaviors that were modeled throughout my life. These were real relationships where he took real care of his customers—at any time of the day or night.

Seeing these behaviors every day of my life from the time I was a young child really impacted the way I developed relationships with other people in my life. With these examples, I am not sure how I could view relationships any other way.

From the time we are very young, we observe the relationships between those around us, and we develop tendencies that will drive the way we develop relationships with others throughout our own lives. We see our parents and how they interact with others both in their work relationships and the relationships with friends and neighbors; we observe people in every aspect of our lives. As we enter school and eventually the workplace, our behaviors are often impacted by the behaviors we have been exposed to.

Usually, people are different in their personal relationships than they are in their professional ones. Personal relationships and friendships are much more giving relationships. They are developed organically, and trust is formed naturally over the course of the relationship. With this trust comes the desire to give to the other person. This type of desire is driven by the purity of the relationship, by truly and sincerely wanting what is best for the other person, your friend. What if we treated all the relationships in our lives in this way—sincerely?

As we grow up and are exposed to different types of relationships, whether we realize it or not, we are taking everything in, and our own behaviors are being programmed. The question is—is this programming going to help you maximize your own personal and professional relationships? After reading this book, I am hopeful you will be challenged to examine the relationships in your life against the examples in the book, which should help to deepen all of the relationships in your life!

Prior to the internet and social media, people would meet other people through more organic means than people often meet today. As I mentioned earlier, the proliferation of social media and e-commerce has impacted everything about the way we live our lives. The means through which people are meeting one another today rarely lend themselves to organically building sincere relationships.

Given the impersonal nature of relationship building today, this book will provide the philosophies and strategies to

build the sincere relationships necessary for maximum personal and professional success.

Most people segment their lives into a personal side and a professional side, and they rarely, if ever, integrate the relationships from the two sides. The biggest reason for this is that this is usually the behavioral modeling we experience from our parents and our bosses. It is also because some people are simply not comfortable mixing the two sides of their lives.

My personal experiences, as well as the experiences of many people I know, have convinced me this is not the way to live one's happiest life. Many people are simply uncomfortable becoming friends with those they meet through business. They "don't want to go there" or they "don't feel it would be appropriate." However, as you will learn in this book, those who allow themselves to blend the two often live the most fulfilled lives and enjoy the most opportunities over time.

THE 360-DEGREE, MULTI-DIMENSIONAL RELATIONSHIP

The relationships we build throughout our lives are often 180-degree, one-dimensional relationships. They are based on either something personal or professional, but usually not both. We keep them on one side of the circle of our lives or the other, and we do not build them into the multidimensional relationships they have the potential to become.

When we first meet new people, they are an acquaintance, whether we meet them through a personal or professional circumstance. Hopefully, they become a friend, and this often happens naturally. How can we turn more acquaintances into friends? From there, how can we turn friends into trusted confidantes? If we have more trusted confidantes, perhaps we can do business with these trusted friends, which makes business much safer and rewarding. Who doesn't want to do business with people they can really trust?

Throughout my career, I have found those who are most successful and fulfilled are the ones who approach all relationships through a 360-degree, multi-dimensional relationship perspective. They consider all aspects of how they might bring value to one's life. Philosophically, everyone they meet is their friend, and they sincerely consider how they can bring value to the other person in the relationship from the very beginning.

In this context, it is absolutely okay to do business, but both sides of the transaction must be sincere and therefore, uncommon value can be unleashed.

For instance, typically, when we meet people for a business transaction, other than a bit of small talk, we usually only address the business situation. It is transactional, even if both sides of that transaction are the nicest, most sincere people in their personal lives. The goal is to be taken sincerely—but how does that happen? You must act sincere; not just say you are sincere. When you act this way, you may not get anything today, but the goodwill you are building for the future is immeasurable and creates tremendous opportunity for the future due to the trust established.

More and more meetings are taking place online, which creates an additional roadblock to creating sincere relationships. Therefore, we need to be more intentional about creating them.

Usually, when a person is selling a product or service, they will try to differentiate based on either the quality of what they represent or the quality of the service they offer. Sometimes they go in a bit of a personal direction, but rarely, if ever, do people take it as far as possible personally—they just don't want to go there. It is important to realize every person one meets from a business perspective is trying to accomplish two basic streams of goals in their lives—their personal and professional.

IF WE CAN HELP PEOPLE TO REALIZE THEIR PERSONAL GOALS, NOT ONLY THEIR GOALS AT WORK, OUR RELATIONSHIPS WILL ONLY DEEPEN
Additionally, by the time you get into a meeting where you are trying to sell something, you are behind the eight ball in terms of creating a sincere relationship simply due to the fact there is money involved. If you are successful in blending and developing a sincerely personal relationship, you will set yourself apart from the rest.

However, this is not easy. The best business deals I have ever done were with people I met before they needed my service. I had already established sincere trust with these folks, and as we move forward in the book, I will provide specifics on how this was accomplished. The message here is when it was time to discuss a business transaction, there was already trust, without which maximum value would simply not have been possible! The others I discuss in the book do the same thing.

On the professional side, if a person meets another person as a potential client or employee, the nature of the relationship is set up from the beginning. Both sides are trying to make something happen—a transaction. If you are hired by a company as an employee, your relationship with your boss is a professional one, not a friendship. Many managers are hesitant to develop friendships with their employees in fear they may need to let them go at some point, or they simply want to maintain professional relationships with those they work with. They might be *friendly*, but they are not your friend. Similarly, many people in sales roles think they have a *relationship* with their customer when they really have a *contact*.

Sincere relationships are more important today than ever; however, tools like LinkedIn have not helped this situation, as many people think the goal is to amass the most LinkedIn connections. The problem with this thinking is if you do not really know these people and they will not return your call, you do not have a relationship.

If you meet someone through them becoming your client, they are your *client and your client only* until they hopefully become your friend. Everyone in sales wants their client to become their friend, and many think their client is their friend, but are they really? This is something I wanted to explore as I went through the journey of writing this book. I wanted to explore how these relationships that are initially one-dimensional become multi-dimensional and mutually beneficial.

When people go to work, they are responsible for creating value for the enterprise that employs them. As people come together in companies, they should work toward a common goal to grow the enterprise effectively and efficiently in a way that aligns with shareholder expectations. When someone is employed, they are expected to do all they can to help the enterprise accomplish its goals. If you or your firm are hired to perform a service through a relationship, a referral, a recruiter, or any other means, your relationship is such that you are expected to contribute to the success of the company and do what you were hired to do.

However, we all have another much more important job. Whether we realize it or not, we all run a small business at home. We need to maintain a steady income over time, and as I will illustrate in this book, the best way to ensure the ability to maintain a steady income is to consistently build sincere *360-degree and multi-dimensional relationships* with others. This will not only be increasingly important to your success, but it will also significantly fulfill your life.

360-DEGREE, MULTI-DIMENSIONAL RELATIONSHIPS AS INSURANCE

As we grow throughout our careers and move into more strategic positions of higher authority, these relationships become more important as an insurance policy to ensure we are exposed to the best possible professional opportunities, resources, and eventual personal friendships.

There are clear strategies I will discuss later in this book that can and should be employed by everyone regardless of where you are in your life and your career.

Unfortunately, today's market is such that most people do not work for the same company for their entire careers. We must create relationships to ensure we protect our careers and our ability to take care of our families.

When I was a kid, the thing I most looked forward to was going to work with my father. As I mentioned earlier, my father has owned a company for over fifty years that sells everything from flour and sugar to fruit filling and muffin batters to large and small bakeries, hotels, and restaurants. He has customers of all shapes and sizes.

As I also said, going to work with him was not the typical "going to work" experience most kids have with their parents. My father did not go to a job at a desk in a stuffy office building. Going to work with my father meant going to see his clients, who as I said were *always* his friends.

My father never separated his business relationships from his personal ones. Everyone was a personal relationship to him. There was no one whose kids and families my dad did not show a sincere interest in, whether it meant remembering birthdays or memorizing their phone numbers. On the weekends, it was these people's children whose birthday parties I attended. I did not realize it at the time, but I was learning the building blocks of building sincere relationships from the ground up. Those experiences would impact everything about the way I lived my life, personally and eventually professionally as well.

My father's company provided products to the best bakeries in Chicago. In fact, there is a bagel base product that is used in many of the bagel shops around the country that to this day is called *Aaron's Bagel Base,* which again goes to show the personal way my father has always done things.

He always woke up for work at 4:00 a.m. Many of his bakery clients worked all night long, and their day would end at sunrise. On days when I would go to work with him, I would always have trouble sleeping the night before, and I would jump out of bed at 4:00 a.m., ready to go. It would always be dark, and when I walked outside, everything had a wonderful, fresh morning smell, as if each day was the beginning of a new life.

Although my father was never a breakfast-eater, he would make sure I was fed when we went to see his customers. This would mean heading to an IHOP on the south side of Chicago or some such place, always in neighborhoods that differed greatly from the one I lived in. Given that my father spent a good amount of his time working, we would have an opportunity to connect and have great conversations.

We would then head out to see his customers. If we walked in through the front of a retail bakery, all the counter people knew him, and he would just walk to the back. If it was more of a wholesale operation, we would just walk through the back door. This seemed normal to me, but it took me a few years to realize this was solely due to the relationships of trust my father successfully built. He walked in like he owned the place, and everyone loved him.

"Hey, Cliff! How are you? Is that your kid? Does he want a cookie or donut?" I heard this every place I went, to such an extent it just seemed regular to me. I thought that was how everyone worked!

My dad would then write the order without the customer's input. He did not have any notes. One time I asked him, "Dad, why don't these customers want to give you their order? Why do they let you do this?"

He said, "Aaron, the truth is I know their business and how quickly they go through products better than they do. They trust me to take the order myself and ship it to them because they know I treat their business as if it were my own."

Over the years, I grew to see just how important this trust was. My father was truly invested in his clients' success. He wanted them to succeed and became a vital part of each client's team just through the way he served them. This was the example my father set for me. To me, this was just the way things were done.

All through my childhood, I was a performer. In 1988, after spending a year and a half as a vocal performance major at the University of Illinois at Urbana-Champaign, I found myself at a significant crossroads. I was on "double secret probation" due to terrible grades that were the result of joining a fraternity, having way too much fun, and rarely, if ever, attending classes. Ultimately, I ended up in a situation where I was in danger of being kicked out of school.

My father, who was financing my schooling, was livid. He made it clear. He said, "I am not paying for you to hang out with your friends and party! Unless you have some way of paying for your next semester in Champaign, you are coming home, and you can look into local colleges."

At the time, I was extremely pissed, as I loved the experiences I was having in school socially. However, I had no idea how to do the educational aspect of college. I simply didn't want to miss out on the fun, but I did not realize in order to have fun in college, one needs to do the work. Didn't they just hand out college degrees as a rite of passage? I learned the answer to this was a hard "no."

I returned to live with my parents, every twenty-year-old's dream place to be. I enrolled at Kendall College in Evanston, Illinois (now located in Chicago) which is a top hospitality management program. In high school, I had worked in numerous restaurants, so I figured this was as good a place as any to start a career. I enjoy people, love sincere relationships, and people always need to eat.

I spent a year at Kendall and did well. It was nice to build confidence that, when I applied myself, I was able to get decent grades. However, I was still pretty uninspired around school.

Any time my father and I discussed school, he always gave the same response: "Why would you go to school when I own a company you are going to run someday? Your family will always be your family."

My father was a tough, street-smart, grizzled man who to me was Superman. He could leap tall buildings in a single bound, he could negotiate anything, and he always had a wad of cash. He made sure we all had everything we needed in life. He was a complete and total people person: tough, but a teddy bear at the same time. He built a business with his partners from scratch, and I respected him.

I decided to leave Kendall College and joined his company. In the next three years, I did most every role, from sweeping floors to selling products to dealing with the bank. I learned a ton. I lived in the city. As I discussed earlier, my father and his partners were some of the greatest networkers and "people" people you will ever meet—they built the business one relationship at a time. People simply wanted to do business with them because they were so sincerely likable, transparent, honest, and just great people to be around. This part of working with my father was amazing.

One afternoon in 1993 or so, I was seeing a concert at Soldier Field in Chicago. My very primitive cell phone rang, and it was one of my customers. At the time, I was running the warehouse and shipping departments for my dad's company.

"Aaron, it's Shirley—do you have a minute?" I let her know I was at a concert but would step out for a moment to talk with her. She let me know she had run out of a very specific flour she needed for the evening's production. Sounds familiar, huh?

I let her know the concert was about to start, but when it was over, I would drive to the warehouse, pick up what she needed, and drop it off to her. This was just how we did things.

A couple of months earlier, I had picked up this account with the promise, in these types of situations, I would be there to take care of them. It was a sincere promise and one I meant.

However, there was much about my father's business I wanted to change and improve. Manufacturing processes were still being done in the same ways they were done in the early 1970s, and I felt in order to take the company to the next level, process improvements were necessary. However, I did not have the background, education, or experience to make these changes a reality. It was extremely frustrating since I knew in order to scale the business, changes needed to be made, but I had no idea how to express these opportunities. I found myself uninspired.

I will never forget walking into my father's office and closing the creaky door behind me. I asked my dad if we could have a serious talk, and I told him I was leaving his company to finish what I had started in college. I could tell he was crushed; after all, his goal was to have his children take over his company. He certainly appreciated my desire to complete my schooling, but he clearly had a hard time coming to terms with this.

One huge benefit of working for my father was he was a long-time season ticket holder for the Chicago Bulls, where he took clients and friends over the years. I have always been a huge basketball fan and would have a great time at these games. I was lucky enough to see Michael Jordan play more times than I can remember (these are stories for a different book).

In 1991, a couple of years prior to the conversation with my father about returning to school, I was headed to a Bulls/Pistons playoff game. I was working for my father at the time. I was excited and had tunnel vision. This was prime Michael Jordan time and the Bulls "needed" to win, which they did, in overtime. After the game, I met up with a good friend and her friend Lisa, and the world changed forever. Lisa and I got engaged three years almost to the day of that meeting.

However, this was not perfect. My family and my soon-to-be wife's family were quite different. Lisa's stepfather (who was extremely successful professionally) felt very strongly that in order to be successful, one needed a very strong education. My father felt one needed "street smarts, relationships, and experience."

I have concluded after many years that the most successful people need both.

After getting married, my father-in-law used pretty much every chance to remind me how much opportunity I might leave on the table by not completing my education. Over time, this not only started to bother me, but it really made me think. Would I be able to support my wife in the way she was used to? Would I be able to support children? What if my father sold the business and I had no transferrable skills? This really concerned me.

"You will never be successful on the path you are on! You will not only need an undergraduate degree from a top school, but you will also need an MBA as well."

This was what I heard from my well-meaning, successful father-in-law in 1991 before eventually marrying the love of my life and now wife of twenty-five years.

At the time, this was tough to hear, but it was hard to argue with the tremendous success he had attained in his life. As someone who wanted to impress his soon-to-be new father-in-law, it turned out to be just the kick in the ass I needed to explore what I needed to complete educationally in order to accomplish my goals. This drove me to have the difficult discussion with my dad and return to school.

When my father-in-law told me I was a failure and I saw the look on his face, I made a decision. I had to find a different type of success. Little did I know what could be possible.

Prior to the meeting with my father, I had kept my thoughts of returning to school entirely to myself, other than a discussion with my wife on our honeymoon.

After spending many years working with my father, I got married to the woman of my dreams in 1995. It had always gnawed at me I had not finished college. I desperately felt the need to finish what I started in the place where I started it.

So, I made the most difficult and best decision of my life six months after getting married. I returned to finish my undergraduate degree at the University of Illinois where, a few years before, I had left to come home to work with my dad.

It was a beautiful sunset dinner on our honeymoon in St. Martin, and my wife had no idea what I was going to say. "Now that we are married, I think I want to return to school," I said. My wife assumed I wanted to attend a local school at night while still working for my father. No, this was not my plan. I wanted her to quit her job at Cartier and I wanted to quit my job with my father, then I wanted us to move to Champaign, Illinois, with our dog.

About a month before our wedding, I got in touch with the Dean of the College of Music at the University of Illinois and took a ride to meet with him. Due to my "double secret probation," in order to return to school, I needed to do so in the Music School—however, I did not want to complete my music degree. The dean found this fascinating. "You mean you want me to give you a space in my school, knowing you are going to leave in a semester?" he said.

"Yes," I said.

"Interesting," he said. "Tell you what. I find you interesting, and your goals noble. You get one semester in my school. Get your grades up and get the fuck out of my school—and I will be watching."

It was around this time I realized how you communicate and build relationships with people can really impact how they treat you and the chances they take on you. After my first semester back in school, I achieved a 4.7/5 grade point average. I was able to prove my ability to be successful in school to myself, and yes, the dean kept an eye on me as he promised!

I also learned to use the relationship skills I had learned in business to build great relationships with my professors. I found this made it much easier to be successful as a student, as it gave me additional access. Since these professors knew me and knew I cared about my education, they would give me the benefit of the doubt when grading assignments, exams, etc.

I returned to school in the College of Liberal Arts and Sciences at the University of Illinois and received an undergraduate degree in history. From the time I arrived back on campus, I knew I wanted to pursue an MBA degree, so I networked with professors and administrators from the MBA Program early in my time on campus.

I found myself in the office of Dr. Paul Magelli, a true force of nature in every sense of the word. Dr. Magelli was a brilliant professor and dean of the college that was a pioneer in graduate school education. He was one of the first to create a consulting group in a college that allowed students to do real work for outside companies. As he learned more about my background and goals, he said to me enthusiastically, "Aaron, you can be an extremely successful MBA student, and we would love to have you in our program." I could not believe I was now a successful student; it felt amazing, and the opportunities felt endless. Having someone like this believe in me was incredible.

He shared with me work the group was doing for Lockheed Martin around the vehicle that was set to replace the space shuttle. I decided then and there I would attend this MBA Program. Paul became a true friend and mentor to me until his death a few years ago. Paul was another from whom I learned the value of building true relationships, finding mentors, and being vulnerable.

Interestingly, I also received acceptance at the DePaul University Kellstadt Graduate School of Business, and they offered me a scholarship. However, due to the clear sincerity of Dr. Magelli, and a feeling I had about him as a potential mentor, I decided to attend the University of Illinois instead. Based on the work I did both academically and for the program itself in the first year, in my second year of the program, I received a ten-thousand-dollar scholarship toward my education. Dr. Magelli was a friend and amazing mentor to me over the years.

After two years in the program, I received an offer to join one of the top consulting firms in the country, Andersen Consulting (currently called Accenture.) I had overcome the challenge of not only earning one degree, but two. I had accomplished getting an offer from a premier firm. I also learned more about how the value of relationships was just as important in "big company corporate America" as it was for my father and his partners, as they developed their business over many years.

In three years, I went from a newly married, non-educated man who had grown up with the examples of building a business through sincere relationships to a consultant at a Big 4 firm who had truly begun to see the benefits that can be created in big-company, corporate America through many of the same behaviors I had already learned. My future was bright.

After I left Accenture, I joined Robert Half International, a large staffing firm. My job was to find clients who needed additional assistance to get work done, both day-to-day work as well as special projects. The job was all about meeting new people and building new relationships.

Since I had worked in Big 4 consulting, I was hired into one of the consulting divisions of the company doing business development. This group goes to market as consultative, but typically conducts business in a pretty transactional way. While the company certainly does good work, the staffing business itself tends to be transactional, not an industry where deep relationships are built. While working for my father, I had worked in sales roles and as noted above, I worked with some of the best relationship people in my father and his partners. I joined Robert Half because I figured the lessons I learned about relationships from my father would transfer well into this business—and it turns out I was right.

My job was to cold-call companies in the area with whom we could do business. These were typically chief financial officers, controllers, chief information officers, etc., of large companies who might need to augment their staff due to special projects, losing staff, or simply needing additional assistance to get work done.

This was exactly the type of job I was at home in. After all, I had grown up watching my father build solid and long-lasting relationships with his clients. I was ready to do the same.

One of the first clients I connected with was the Vice President of Internal Audit at a company in Deerfield, Illinois, called Dade Behring. Lou Fernandez invited me to see him in his office to get to know one another.

At the time, I was early in my career in professional services selling. For this reason, I was required to attend this meeting with my boss. We met with Lou and discussed his potential need for assistance in complying with the Sarbanes-Oxley Act. This was 2003, right after the Enron scandal rocked public companies and the US Securities and Exchange

Commission [SEC] said registered companies needed to comply with requirements they had never needed to comply with in the past. Most companies did not have the resources to keep up with all the work that was required to comply with this new law. Therefore, they would turn to different types of professional services firms to assist them in providing additional people to assist in getting the work done. These would be accounting firms, staffing firms, and consulting firms, all of whom would provide additional professionals to help get the work completed. Given the deadlines, it was very difficult to find resources with the appropriate backgrounds to get this work done at the time.

As someone who had grown up professionally at the Big 4 accounting firm PricewaterhouseCoopers, Lou had a bias for utilizing true professional services firms that would provide their own employees over staffing firms that provided contract labor. My firm was the latter; however, Lou was willing to give me and my firm a chance based on the quality of the initial meeting. Interestingly, over the years since, we have discussed the reasons Lou was willing to give me a chance. It is something one can't put their finger on, but when one is being sincere, you can often feel it, and this was the case in this meeting on both sides. As we worked together and built a trusting relationship, we were able to prove together it is as much about *how* you do something as *what* you happen to be doing. This was proven by the fact that over time, Lou did more and more business with me and less and less with my competitors.

Over the next year or so, I learned a ton about internal audit from my new friend Lou. We got together socially, went to a Cubs game, and had a couple of lunches as well. We discussed our families and our kids, and we became friends. The more I learned about the business and what Lou needed to do to comply with Sarbanes-Oxley, the better I became at taking care of him professionally.

A bit into our relationship, as we were having lunch, I mentioned my young son needed to build a Pinewood Derby car for Cub Scouts and I had no idea how to help him.

"My son and I won every single Pinewood Derby we participated in. Why don't you and your son come over to my house and we will build a car?" Lou said.

A couple of weeks later, my son Andrew and I went to Lou's house and built an incredible competitive car. We had a tremendous afternoon together and more of a real relationship was formed. A 360-degree, multi-dimensional relationship!

At one of our meetings, Lou pulled out his audit plan, which included details on all the work that needed to be done over the next few months, where in the world the work needed to take place, and the type of audit that was needed, which would indicate the background of the professional/s I needed to provide. Lou stated to me, rather than calling me each time he needed assistance, he would like me to simply provide him the professionals who were needed to do this work on the dates outlined on his plan. This was a turning point in our professional relationship, as it showed we reached a level of trust that wasn't typical for a standard client relationship. Normally, staffing firms are not trusted in this way, but because of *how* I had worked with him, Lou had grown to see me as a trusted partner. He did not need to meet the consultants I was providing to confirm their fit. He trusted I understood him and his needs well enough and I would not do anything for a "transaction" today that might jeopardize his work or our long-term relationship.

While in a different industry, these were the same dynamics my father had with his friends and clients, *and this was when I realized I was truly onto something special.*

Over the years, Lou and I have stayed in close touch and become even better friends. When he has been in career transition, I have created countless introductions for him. After he remarried, my wife and I got to know his new wife Erika and eventually his new daughter Madeleine. The relationship came to transcend business—however, we still found opportunities to do business together.

During the COVID-19 pandemic, I found myself in a relationship management/business development role at Baker Tilly in Chicago, a large consulting/CPA firm I had been with for almost eight years—a great run. Given the impact of COVID-19 to business, I left the firm to work on my book and to reassess where I belonged professionally to make the biggest impact in people's lives and for their companies. So much had changed in my career, and it was a great time to reassess.

Lou had joined a very differentiated company called Compass Marketing Incorporated out of Annapolis, Maryland, as their controller/CFO. Compass partners with its consumer-packaged goods clients in creating sustainable, quantifiable, and differentiated business value over time for companies of all sizes. As an Amazon Advertising partner,

Compass has a long history of "winning the buy button," along with the hearts and minds of consumers for the world's greatest brands—basically helping their clients to sell more and drive more revenue. The services are very differentiated and not at all a commodity.

In practical language, this means Compass represents large and small brands and helps them sell more of their products on Amazon and other e-commerce channels, as well as in "brick and mortar" stores. These could be well-established brands or newer, start-up brands—it is a tremendous business with a tremendous future. After all, who doesn't want to grow their business?

Lou and I got into a conversation about my network, the differentiated offerings of Compass that allow companies to grow their brands in today's digital world and sell more profitably and predictably, and the companies in Chicago they felt they might be able to assist. He sent me a spreadsheet of potential companies. After taking a look, I knew there were people I knew personally who would potentially be interested in the Compass value proposition. These relationships were in large part due to the behaviors I outline throughout this book.

I didn't just know these folks; they would return my call.

Lou suggested I have a conversation and get to know the president of Compass, a thirty-one-year-old Colgate-Palmolive veteran who had been brought into the company a year prior, given the explosive growth of the company. After an hour-long call, during which we completed one another's sentences, he said to me, "In talking with Lou, I could tell you take incredible care of your clients and treat them as if they are family, and I thought this is a skill set we need at Compass as we grow. However, your background on paper does not lend itself to representing our value proposition. After having a chance to talk with you, I truly feel you could be an amazing asset to our organization."

If it had not been for my long-time relationship with Lou, this conversation would have never taken place!

From there, I went onto a couple other conversations with senior leadership. Two weeks later, I found myself with a life-changing opportunity to join Compass as Vice President of Strategic Accounts.

Bottom line—if it had not been for the 360-degree, multi-dimensional relationship Lou and I had maintained over the years, most likely both of our careers would have turned out differently. I would not have had the amazing opportunity to take the next step in my career at a time when I was clearly ready for that next step. Given the trusting relationship we had built, on joining Compass, there was much less risk for both of us and our companies, as we knew exactly what we were getting as we worked together.

The lessons here are clear: if we sincerely invest ourselves in the success of others, we will build the types of relationships that will make all types of things possible. Lou and I have both benefited tremendously from our 360-degree relationship. It is truly mutually beneficial, and the more of these types of relationships we build in our lives, the better our lives will be.

CHAPTER 3

How Do People Typically Approach Relationships in Business and in Life (and Why Might It Need to Change?)

———

Can I let you in on a little secret? There is one thing you definitely have to have in order to enjoy long-term and sustainable success both personally and professionally—sincerity. But what does sincerity really mean, and how do we accomplish it? Are you truly sincere? Do you even believe real sincerity is possible outside of the relationships you have with your good friends and family?

As I have spoken with people over the years about their attitudes toward forming new relationships, I have found many people are jaded and seem to not believe truly authentic relationships are possible. Everyone must have an agenda, right? I am here to tell you this is not the case.

The year was 1991, and I was working for my father's company. Basically, we manufactured and distributed anything a bakery might need. Given my father owned the company, I grew up programmed to think I could sincerely help any bakery I saw.

At the time, a small natural food grocery chain was expanding into Chicago after only having stores in one state and a couple of stores in neighboring states. They were embarking on a strategy to expand across the country, and one of the first cities they opened in was Chicago. One day, I saw this awesome new store with amazing signage and a message that was all about health, and I decided to check it out.

From the minute I walked into the store, I was blown away. From the initial smell to the way they displayed their inventory to the quality, it was clear this was much more than your average grocery store. Of course, one of the first things I wanted to check out was the bakery. It was amazing, with breads and pastries that almost jumped out of the case and into your senses, that was how good they looked and smelled. I asked to meet the bakery manager.

From the back emerged a guy around my age wearing a black concert shirt and an apron covered in flour, clearly in the middle of the day's production. He had a huge smile on his face as he reached out his hand to say hello.

I explained I was in the "business" and was truly impressed by the store, and the bakery specifically. He explained he had recently moved to Chicago to open this store. As we discussed a bit more about their expansion strategy, he explained they planned to open more stores in the Midwest. As we talked, it occurred to me to ask where he buys his supplies.

"That is a great question," he said. "Because we have virtually no space to store anything, we get the supplies we need for the day's baking every morning and we pay a substantial amount in delivery fees. We are trying to figure out a different strategy as this is clearly not sustainable."

Realizing I had a huge warehouse half a mile away, I offered to store products for him and deliver them to him each day since we had trucks going out anyway. I explained this would clearly be less expensive for him, and I wasn't worried about what my company made on this. It was clear to me to explore how we could sincerely create a situation for him that was better than the one he currently had—it just made sense, sincere sense.

We set up a time to meet again, and he shared his entire list of what he was buying. We discussed how we could sell him these items and deliver them from our local warehouse. I was completely transparent about pricing, and we started to do a bit of business. Today, it is thirty years later and my father and his company still enjoy an amazing relationship with him. I truly do not think this would have taken place had the relationship not had a beginning where it was clear I just wanted to sincerely help—and was able to sincerely bring value.

The goal must be to meet and develop relationships with people who don't bring an agenda into every new relationship—but how do we do this, and how do we gauge who is real and who isn't? It is not in words; it is in actions. Actions cannot be faked.

Throughout our lives, we develop relationships with other human beings for many reasons. We crave relationships with others in order to live our best lives both personally and professionally. Without relationships, life would be boring, and it would be difficult to create value for the world. We require relationships to get a job, keep a job, create business opportunities, get married, have children, and so many other things that bring us joy and create value in the world.

As one really thinks about it, the ability to develop and maintain relationships with others is one of the most important skills we develop as people. How well you are able to navigate relationships throughout your life will in large part determine the quality of your life, both personally as well as professionally.

When most people are asked what they are looking for in life, it often comes down to one word—happiness. In general, we desire satisfaction in our lives, and to have more pleasant than unpleasant experiences. Losing a job, for example, is a very negative experience. What are some ways we can minimize negative and maximize positive experiences?

Researchers at the University of Virginia have proposed another dimension of wellbeing they are currently studying. They refer to this as *psychological richness.*[7]

---

7   Kira Newman et al., "The Top 10 Insights from the "Science of a Meaningful Life" in 2020," Greater Good Magazine, December 17, 2020.

This concept involves being exposed to new ideas and experiences that are interesting. It can also involve meeting others who expose you to these new and interesting experiences. If you are someone who exposes others to these new experiences, you will be perceived in the sincere way you intend.

In a paper published in *Affective Science,* researchers from the University of Virginia asked people from nine countries to journal about their ideal life. After this activity, they were asked to analyze it in terms of how happy, meaningful, or psychologically rich it was. The ideal life they envisioned tended to be very happy and meaningful, but also surprisingly moderately "eventful, interesting, and surprising;" in other words, psychologically rich. [8]

When people were asked to choose between the three types of lives, most chose a happy or meaningful life; 7 to 17 percent chose a psychologically rich life.

To take this even further, they surveyed people from the United States and Korea about their biggest regret. The results of this were 28 percent of Americans and 35 percent of Koreans said their lives would be psychologically richer (rather than happier of more meaningful) if they could undo this regret, which suggests psychological richness is an important goal in their lives. How do we accomplish this? We can certainly create interesting lives for ourselves through the development of sincere relationships.

---

8   Ibid.

Some who are reading this might think it sounds like, "I need to be an extrovert to do this all successfully and I am not an extrovert, so this will be very uncomfortable for me." Some might be tempted to close the book and never open it again—*don't*.

You do not need to be an extrovert to be successful with the suggestions in this book! Many of the best relationship builders are not extroverts—they are introverts. However, *they act like extroverts*. That is all it takes.

You do not have to be comfortable in front of a large group of people or cold-calling people. You do not have to send out blind invites on LinkedIn, hoping people accept your invitation. You simply need to be yourself, help people connect with others, make it clear you would like to meet folks who are of like mind, keep your word, and follow through on your promises.

As children, our parents told us how to behave: listen to teachers, be nice to other kids, share toys, and be good people. Hopefully, this is how our parents were with friends and family, but is this how our parents behaved in business? As I have described, this is how my father behaved and was all I ever saw—but these sincere behaviors are simply not always rewarded at work.

More to the point, is this how *you* operate in business? Do you operate differently in your personal relationships than in your professional ones? Have you ever considered why?

In our personal lives, we approach relationships very sincerely as we look to build friendships, find a spouse, have children, and in general make more friends throughout our lives. We behave kindly, we listen intently, we offer sincere advice and guidance, and when appropriate, we sincerely offer to help. We develop multi-dimensional relationships. Due to the trust established in these relationships, we are taken as we intend. These relationships are not transactions— that is to say, they are not set up due to one side of the relationship owing something to or expecting something from the other side.

Throughout my own life and career, there have been many times when I met people and sincerely wanted to help them; however, it is somewhat human nature to be suspect of other human beings' intentions. These situations can be frustrating. It is like there is an artificial roadblock set from helping others. If we can create more relationships of trust, we will be taken as we truly intend more easily. This can be accomplished by sincerely giving first, instead of waiting for the other party to do so.

Personal relationships develop organically, and we all enjoy these types of relationships in different facets of our lives. They tend to be sincere and pure. As we develop these friendships, we sincerely care about those we develop these natural relationships with. This allows us to develop authentic bonds with other people we can rely on throughout our lives.

If we think about our longtime, personal, *real* friends, we know for the most part these people really have our back. These sincere relationships are ones we as human beings are naturally drawn to. When we identify things we have in common with others and look to give first without knowing what we might get, these bonds form even more quickly, as illustrated in the grocery store example above. These can be family, people we met in school, in college, or through business—the context of our relationships doesn't matter as much as the bond of trust. *You can feel when you can truly trust another person.*

Interestingly, there is science behind this as well. As I mentioned, human beings are social animals who thrive on connections with others. Research has shown both the quality and quantity of an individual's social relationships can significantly affect his or her mental health, physical health, and mortality risk. Those with more intimate and extended social networks tend to live longer and have fewer health complications than those who are more solitary. The influence of emotional health on our physical health is truly incredible and is something we will continue to learn more about.[9]

Also, when we meet people through our friends, we trust them more immediately as opposed to when meeting a stranger. This is only natural, of course, but the implications on your professional life are huge! If you consistently get to know people and maintain relationships throughout your career, the world becomes incredibly small—which is very good when you are trying to make business happen.

Have you ever considered what this means for the quality of your life, and how you should intentionally meet and work with others and manage relationships in your life?

---

9   Charlotte Hu, "Demystifying Love: The Science Behind Human Relationships," Dailybreak, June 27, 2017.

We all want to find more relationships with those we can trust, but how do we find more of these relationships of sincere trust?

APPROACH ALL RELATIONSHIPS AS FRIENDSHIPS

What if we approached business relationships the same way we approached friendships? What if we thought of those we work with as friends who we sincerely look out for and want to help, and we authentically celebrated their success and looked to help them reach it? What if we took action to assist these folks in the same way we do our personal friends?

By far, the best business deals I have done throughout my career have been with people I knew prior to trying to "sell them something." I have found in order to be taken as I intend in looking to create sincere business value, there must be sincere trust established first. This is also the case when moving through one's career; the more trust one can establish over time with those they get to know, the better the opportunities will be that come to them over time.

A couple of years ago, I was introduced to a very high-level, senior executive at a large company in the Chicago area. He was the type of person who anyone in my industry would want to know, as he represented a "buyer of services." I have found people at this level are often skeptical of new relationships, as they do not wish to be "sold to." However, these same people are very open to "buying well" from those they trust. These people know bullshit when they see it.

I was introduced as someone who had a network that might be able to assist him either personally or professionally. I was warned he was very direct and to the point. He would not mince words. I was looking forward to meeting him.

We set an in-person meeting for a half hour. An hour and a half later, we were still talking. To this day, we are good friends and we have indeed done business together. The question is: what was different about the beginnings of this relationship that led to significant trust quite quickly? I recently asked him this question.

"From the moment we sat down, it was clear your intent was not to sell anything. It was clear you were more interested in getting to know me and to add real value over time—and that can't be faked. Therefore, I was more open to hearing about a differentiated business model. Since that time, you have delivered on the initial promise and added value in every interaction."

In that initial meeting, I learned more about his career and his goals. Beyond the goals he had at his current company, I was able to understand more about his holistic, personal, and professional goals as well. From there, I thought about my personal/professional network to determine who in my network might be of assistance to him over time. I offered to make those introductions and I followed through on my promises. They were all impressive people in their own right and it opened our relationship to discuss the unique value proposition I could present to his company.

If it had not been for the initial trust that was established, there would not have been an opportunity to present the unique value proposition of my company and to create a personal/professional relationship that was actually sustainable.

Today's market is not a market where old-school, traditional sales prospecting really works. It is a market where, if you want to build and maintain a fulfilled and progressive career, building authentic relationships and friendships is increasingly important. Decision makers do not answer the phone, and when they do and perceive they are being sold to, they shut down. The decision makers you want to know tend to have a bullshit meter that serves them quite well.

In today's world of marketing automation and online selling, people still crave sincere connections.

The goal when meeting people should be to *connect* rather than *convert*.

Converting is transactional and cold, whereas *connecting* is long-term, warm, and will keep your clients with you for the long haul while turning them into sincere friends!

The approach to new business relationships is typically sterile, even when people think they are being sincere. Despite good intentions, from a professional perspective, people tend to meet other people through a job interview, a business deal, or some other transaction. So how does one accomplish developing sincere professional relationships when these relationships are set up to be impersonal?

I wondered that same thing myself over the years, and author Adam Grant gives some insight into this in his book *Give and Take*. He talks about three types of people: Givers, Takers, and Matchers.

HOW CAN YOU BE A GIVER AND STILL BE SUCCESSFUL?

Givers look to give more into a relationship; they do not come into relationships looking to get something from the other side. They sincerely are looking for ways to "give" to the other party, and they follow through with their promises to others. As they do this both initially and over time, a true relationship is formed. Matchers look for more of an equal exchange of favors, a quid pro quo where one wonders who will give first. Takers look to take from the relationship and do not look to provide anything into it for anyone other than themselves.[10]

Two obvious questions come up whenever you assess whether you are a Giver, Matcher, or Taker. The first is how to be a Giver and still find success. The second is whether it really matters. After all, plenty of Takers out there are enjoying the success you and I both want—at least monetary success—but is that what life is about?

Is that success sustainable over the long term? Can they build on that transactional success to build a great personal and professional life?

---

10   Adam Grant, *Give and Take: A Revolutionary Approach to Success* (New York: Penguin Group, 2013)

To answer the first question, people naturally trust Givers. Givers are people who truly care as much about the success of others as they do about their own success, even more so. Grant defines Givers at work as the supportive people who enjoy sharing their expertise and helping the careers of others. Givers tend to develop 360-degree, multi-dimensional relationships.

They share their networks and business contacts and give their time to mentoring people. Interestingly, studies by Grant have found the least successful people are the Givers. Salespeople who spend their time helping others often close the least amount of sales; engineers who get the least amount of work done often are those who spend the most time assisting others; etc. In medical school, he found the worst grades often went to students who most agreed with statements such as "I like helping others."

The question then becomes, why would one want to be a Giver? As one would expect, Grant's research also found the least successful people are Takers. Takers sometimes find short-term success; however, the Matchers always catch up with them as Matchers enjoy nothing more than exposing Takers. In order to find long term success, being a Giver of some sort is necessary. In terms of looking at companies, Grant found giving companies perform better in every single category, from employee retention to client satisfaction to revenue growth. The most successful organizations are those that foster a giving culture. However, it is important these organizations realize the Givers in their organizations are their greatest asset. Givers are humble and inspire those around them. They are not afraid to ask for help, and they foster and lead organizations where asking for help is just a part of the day-to-day culture. In many companies, people do not feel it is safe to ask questions, and Grant found these types of organizations underperform over time.[11]

So in order to be a Giver and be successful, you must find ways of building mutually beneficial relationships with those you meet over the course of your career. You must find ways of doing small things for people who have the potential to bring tremendous value.

I'll remind you of the statistic 60 percent of people get jobs with people they know, and this number is only getting larger. In the course of my career, I have found those who enjoy the greatest happiness and success in their careers are those who are working with people they know and truly trust.

If one is a C-level executive, the company typically only has one; CFO, CEO, COO, etc. Therefore, there are less of these jobs in the marketplace, and more people competing for them. Company leaders and corporate boards manage their risk in terms of who they hire and will always go with talent who is familiar to them, or talent who knows someone they know and trust. The higher up you progress in your field, the more important relationships are going to be. Sure, there may be outliers, but the best way to ensure success is to lean into sincere relationships, not away from them.

Therefore, having the most "connections" on LinkedIn might not be the recipe for success. Rather, you should look at your

---

11   *TED*, "Adam Grant: Are You a Giver or a Taker?" January 24, 2017, video, 13:28.

connections and really consider which of these people you really know and which make sense to get to know better in order to maintain long-term happiness, as well as career and personal success. Find the Givers and take great care of them, and don't be afraid to accept help yourself.

CREATE A NETWORK OF FRIENDS, NOT JUST CONNECTIONS

Do you simply have a network of connections, or are they real relationships?

It used to be that some of this Giver mentality came more naturally to people because in order to do business, you were required to get to know other people in a physical sense. In today's marketplace, more and more business is done through online channels, and this is creating a more impersonal business world.

However, people still hire other people. People still make decisions about which firms or service providers to hire. While machines will often sift through resumes, actual human beings make the final buying and hiring decisions. It therefore makes sense as a proactive strategy to spend time fostering better, deeper relationships with those we work with, and to be open to having business-related conversations with those we know personally if it means we can sincerely help them.

To illustrate this, let's consider a common role that crosses all industries—sales. Regardless of what someone is selling, they need to have a relationship of some sort with their buyer.

Every salesperson wants their client to see them as sincere; however, this is becoming more and more difficult.

What most salespeople do not realize is just taking care of their client's needs is not enough to develop a sincere relationship, as this is often not personal to them as human beings, unless they happen to own the company. It is important to go deeper and to do this sincerely. Those who are successful in developing sincere relationships take a true interest in other people as human beings—and people know the difference between those who are sincere and those who are putting on a show.

Consider the story above. In the two years since I met the decision maker I mentioned, our relationship has evolved significantly. At one point, a couple of months after meeting, he gave me a call and let me know he wanted to discuss a project. We got together and discussed how my firm could help his company accomplish the goals of the project. When he called me to let me know my firm had won the work over other firms that had a more recognized name, this is what he said:

"We are awarding you the work, first of all, because your firm clearly has the technical expertise to do the work well. However, most importantly, it is because I trust you to make sure the work is done well. If this project goes well, it can be very good for my career at my company, and if it does not, it would not be a good thing."

I was certainly happy to win the work, but more importantly, it was a testament to the fact that:

People dislike *being sold to*. They are very open to *buying well*, and they will buy from those they *sincerely trust*, not just those they like.

In order to help people buy well, they need to trust you first, and real trust is not just given away, it is earned. Throughout the rest of this book, you will read stories of people who have established sincere trust with people throughout their lives, many with whom they have done tremendous business deals over the years.

The role of salesperson has changed and continues to change. According to the Bureau of Labor Statistics, there are roughly nine million people in non-retail sales roles in the United States. It is safe to assume most learn how to sell through on-the-job training from their mentors and managers. Interestingly, according to a recent HubSpot study, salespeople spend just one-third of their day actually talking to prospects. They spend 21 percent of their day writing e-mails, 17 percent entering data, another 17 percent prospecting and researching leads, 12 percent going to internal meetings, and 12 percent scheduling calls. This leaves only 21 percent of their time to actually develop real relationships with clients and prospects.[12]

This opens up huge opportunity for those who can find ways of doing these other things more efficiently (or not doing them at all), therefore allowing more time for developing real

---

12 Mimi An, "How Salespeople Learn," *HubSpot* (blog), December 11, 2019, accessed January 23, 2021.

relationships. Additionally, organizations need to consider this breakdown and provide their salespeople more time to build authentic and sincere relationships in order for these organizations to set themselves apart from their competition and create the best possible customer experience, and to eventually grow and maintain revenue.

If you take great care of another person regardless of whether that person is a client, friend, server in a restaurant, or any other person you come into contact with throughout your life and think about how you would want to be treated in a friendship, you will find the relationships you are developing will only deepen. Regardless of whether or not your professional role is in sales, these same relationship dynamics apply.

CHAPTER 4

Why Do Sincere Relationships Always Matter?

"People do business with people they like."

UNKNOWN

Have you ever heard this before, or at least something along these lines? People love to say this, and while this is true, *trust* is actually more important when it comes to who people do business with, who they hire, who they become friends with, and with whom they develop relationships in general.

As human beings, we naturally do the things we enjoy doing first and leave the things we do not enjoy or come harder to us until later. Furthermore, we gravitate to the people we not only like, but who we trust as well. For instance, there are some people who I enjoy spending time with and may get a kick out of, but I may not choose to do business with these folks since I do not trust them. Thankfully, I have learned some lessons over the years that relate to this and help me minimize my risk in terms of finding sincere people to get to know and with whom to do business.

While I was in college, I worked as a server for a few different restaurants. For the most part, I enjoyed those I worked with and for; however, I did not always trust them to have my best interest at heart. Restaurants are social and those who work together often socialize together. I became friends with the management team at one restaurant, and at one point, the workload in my classes ramped up. I explained I needed to work fewer shifts, but still wanted to work. They indicated this was "no problem," and for the first couple of weeks I indeed had fewer shifts on the schedule. The third week, when I checked, I had no shifts, and no one had ever discussed this with me.

I went to the general manager, who I thought was my friend, and asked what was up.

"Your availability changed, so I had no choice but to take you off the schedule for now," he said. I explained no one had even mentioned this was possible, and that I certainly needed a couple of shifts each week. I further explained if I knew they might take me off the schedule, I would have had an opportunity to figure out how to make the shifts work. Since I was not informed, I had no chance to restructure my schedule. I was quite upset.

After leaving and taking a few minutes to gather my thoughts, I jumped into my Toyota Camry and I headed to the nicest restaurant in town—Kennedy's. This was a place that was definitely a step up from the place I had been working, and if I was able to get a waiter job there, I would make more money.

I walked through the front door and asked to talk with the manager. Out came a tall, blonde, serious-looking woman in a business suit. She looked like she was extremely professional. I extended my hand and told her why I was there. "Until a few minutes ago, I worked across town, and due to my availability, I was taken off the schedule. I have tremendous server credentials and references, and I would love to talk with you about waiting tables here. This is by far the nicest place in town."

She looked at my resume for a moment, turned to me, and said, "Your timing is perfect. Can you start on Thursday evening?"

I started on Thursday and things could not have gone better. I made more money, had an even better relationship with my boss, and we ended up becoming real friends.

A few weeks later, I got a call from the manager at the first restaurant. He explained a customer had come in and demanded I work a party for him. A couple of months before, a heavy metal band had played in town; the manager came in with a couple of people for a late-night meal and I waited on them. This guy was right out of central casting, complete with a huge beard, black concert t-shirt, and multiple backstage laminates around his neck from many nights on the road. We had a tremendous time; he asked for my name and we developed a bit of a relationship. They were coming back to town and wanted to have a party, and they wanted me to work the party.

I explained I had already gotten another job at Kennedy's, was honestly making more money, and apologized I could not come back to work the party. I also explained, had they handled it differently and just communicated openly rather than just taking me off the schedule, things might have been different. However, I now had trouble trusting him and the other managers of that restaurant.

A lot of this comes down to maturity and being willing to communicate openly and honestly. Sincerity is not always about communicating positive information. It is about creating relationships with others where it is safe to share both positive and negative information with the other party in the relationship. After all, things do not always go as planned in any relationship, and the difference is often in how it is handled.

COMMUNICATE OPENLY AND HONESTLY—ALWAYS

It is not important to be an extrovert; however, acting like one can take you a very long way. Being willing to have a difficult conversation is also important. This reminds me of a friend I met around fifteen years ago while he was in transition as a controller in Chicago. I meet people like this often, and I assist them with meeting people and understanding the process of networking. When I met him, it was clear to me he was an introvert, but once he got to know me, he totally opened up.

As we got to know one another, we realized we both love Neil Young, and he realized he did not need to become a different person to be successful. He simply needed to be himself, be open to meeting new people, open up to them, look to help them, and stay in touch. It is an amazing formula and it is completely sincere.

A couple of years ago, he moved to a new city due to his wife's new job. This gave him an opportunity to completely reinvent himself and build a completely new network. He attended events, met people, connected people to others, and his network grew in both quantity and, more importantly, quality. He found his sincere network!

In terms of creating new relationships, as we get older, most people do not do these things. They rarely look to proactively develop new relationships either personally or professionally, preferring to stick with the relationships they know and are comfortable with. This is especially true with people who are or who consider themselves to be introverts.

However, there is a cautionary tale to be told here.

The date was September 11, 2001, and it was a normal day. I woke up, dialed into my modem to check the news on Yahoo. com (yes, you still needed to dial in in those days), and saw a plane had crashed into the World Trade Center. It was not reported yet how serious it was and to be honest, I did not think much about it before taking the dog for a walk, taking a shower, and jumping on my bike for my commute to work. At that time, I lived on the north side of Chicago and was working on an internal consulting project for Accenture, which meant I was able to work locally and did not have to travel like many of my associates. I made it a practice to listen to the news on my ride, and on this day, what I heard about a mile into my ride was horrifying. One of the World Trade Center Twin Towers had fallen. I stopped my bike and called my wife, who told me her father was at Chicago Tribune Headquarters and had news that had not hit the wire yet. He wanted me home. Our country was under attack.[13]

"Aaron, David is at Tribune Tower and he is seeing some news come in before it is reported. He wants you home—now! No tall buildings downtown!" My wife was frantically telling me over the phone before I quickly pedaled home to watch the horror play out on the news.

The impact on the American economy was extreme. During 2001 and 2002, employers reported 507 extended mass layoff events that were either directly or indirectly related to the terrorist attacks of September 11, 2001. The layoffs involved 145,844 workers in thirty-four states.

Forty-nine percent of these layoffs and fifty-four percent of the separations occurred in just five States—California, Washington, Nevada, Illinois, and New York.[14]

While the economy bounced back relatively quickly, supported by a relatively resilient American economy as well as aid from the federal government, companies were more careful about who they were hiring, the firms with whom

---

13   Gordon Donovan, "9/11: Then and now — 18 years later," *Yahoo! News*, September 10, 2019.

14   "Extended Mass Layoffs and the 9/11 Attacks," US Bureau of Labor Statistics, accessed January 23, 2021.

they were doing business, and sincere relationships became more important.

Many companies looked at the money they were spending with consulting firms through a very close lens. "Overall, [the attacks] have had a negative impact," said Brad Smith, director of research at Kennedy Information, Inc., which tracked the consulting industry. Clients who were already pausing projects were "canceling, because there are so many more variables involved," he said.[15]

At the time, I was a consultant with Accenture, at a level where I was not responsible for selling the work; rather, my job involved doing the work that was sold by the partners of the firm. However, this was the first time I began to realize the importance of sincere relationships in a professional firm like Accenture, since the firm was feeling the pressure of canceled projects as well as delayed new projects. I saw the partners who were most successful were those who were the most relationship-oriented.

It was just as important for me to build strong internal relationships with partners as it had been for my father to maintain the relationships he had developed with his clients over the years. It was these partners of the firm who decided who was placed onto client projects. The only way to maintain employment was to stay billable on client engagements.

The sincere relationships I had developed with partners turned out to be extremely important to staying staffed on

15   Rachel Emma Silverman, "Accenture Posts 4th-Quarter Loss, Plans Charge Related to Attacks," *Wall Street Journal,* October 12, 2001.

interesting engagements due to the fact the partners would request certain people on their teams.

The truth is, most of my peers simply came to work, did the work that was assigned to them, and went home. They did not network with partners, they did not seek out mentors inside and outside the firm, and they allowed the inertia of the firm to guide their careers.

This strategy works—*until it doesn't*.

When there is plenty of business and the economy is booming, there is plenty of business to go around. When business becomes scarce, relationships become that much more important, and many people wait until they *need* relationships to build them. By that time, it is often too late.

Another example is the economic disaster of 2008 which some have called "The Great Recession," which occurred due to a high default rate and resulting foreclosures of mortgage loans, particularly adjustable-rate mortgages. This crisis created an unemployment rate that peaked at 10 percent, close to double the rate prior to the crisis.[16] Most people were living their lives, working their jobs, not realizing what was to come. Suddenly, twice the number of people were unemployed in the United States almost overnight. Again, sincere relationships became extremely important; as in many cases, those who developed sincere relationships determined the difference between those who lost their jobs and those who did not.

---

16 "BLS Spotlight on Statistics: The Recession of 2007–2009," US Bureau of Labor Statistics, accessed March 4, 2021.

As I mentioned previously, by that time, I had enjoyed great success selling project consulting services for a couple of different firms, and just prior to the recession in 2008, the firm I worked for was acquired by another firm. I was regularly contacted by recruiters who would find my information on LinkedIn, and I decided to accept a role for significantly more money, working for people I did not know well—*this was a huge mistake.*

On the day I resigned, I sat down with the president of our division and he said, "Are you sure you want to make this move? We would love you to stick around but understand if you feel you need to move on."

This was someone I had gotten to know well both personally as well as professionally, and therefore this was a very difficult conversation. I was only leaving for the promise of more money, and I was leaving to work with people I did not know well at all.

As the economy tanked, the company I joined let people go around me, leaving me quite exposed in a way I would not have been at my prior company.

BUILD REAL AND SINCERE FRIENDSHIPS AT WORK!
When you build *sincere* and *real* relationships with those you work with and for, they are much more likely to have your back when times get tough.

One day, while sitting at my desk, my phone rang. It was my boss and the guy who had hired me—the only one I trusted in the company—telling me he had been let go. I had a feeling I knew what would take place from there.

I was now reporting to people I had never met who had nothing to do with hiring me. To say they were not nice was an understatement—they were actually mean. Not only did I not have a sincere relationship with these people, but I had virtually no relationship at all.

Given that the people I was now reporting to were clearly not the types of people with whom I could develop a sincere, mutually beneficial relationship, I decided I was not going to stay with the company. I had already begun to network throughout my career to develop business in different sales roles, so I had some sincere relationships to contact in order to begin identifying different potential opportunities. One of those was someone I had tried to recruit a couple of years prior who worked for a competitor firm I had a great deal of respect for. Since I already knew Jim, and we talked every couple of months to catch up, he was aware of the success I had throughout my career.

Although his firm was on a 100 percent hiring freeze, due to our relationship and his awareness of my ability to be successful quickly, he was willing to pass my resume on to his management team and suggest they should talk with me.

"Aaron, given your past success and your network of great relationships, even though we aren't hiring, my boss should still meet you, and I will tell him to!" This was what Jim said to me before putting himself out there to make this meeting happen. Again, without building the sincere relationship, staying in touch with Jim, even though there was no transaction to take place, I would not have had an opportunity to meet with management.

Therefore in the middle of "The Great Recession," I was able to quickly pivot into a role with a highly respected firm through someone I knew well, had met through business, and with whom I had built a significant mutually beneficial relationship.

I am not sure if there is a better example of a time when sincere relationships were more important than during the COVID-19 pandemic of 2020. As I mentioned earlier, in March of that year, the US and global economy was basically shut down, millions of people lost their jobs in all segments of the economy. Those who could work (or had to work) in any type of public environment were doing so while subjecting themselves to substantial risk and no one could leave their homes for much else other than essentials.

When most people think of building sincere relationships, they think about personal, in-person interactions; however, this was impossible. It was the perfect storm—people were losing their jobs left and right, and there was virtually no way to network for new roles in the physical sense of the word.

It was at that time I left the role I was in and started work on this book. In the first month of COVID-19, I must have had literally hundreds of conversations with senior-level executives about the challenges of networking during a global pandemic.

"One of the biggest challenges I am having right now is I am unable to attend in-person events to get to know people," said one of my senior executive friends in March 2020, right after his private equity-backed company was sold. He was in the market looking for a next opportunity and had always networked to make this happen. However, how was he able to do this being stuck at home? Due to the fact he had spent his entire career employed, had done very little networking, and built few relationships outside of the companies in which he worked; he did not have a network to fall back on. He was one of the many, many people in my network who found themselves significantly impacted by this perfect storm.

To fill this void, I decided to set up a virtual executive-level connections group, invite fifteen of my senior executive friends from the Chicago area, and facilitate weekly discussions for this group of people, while also giving them a venue through which to meet others during the pandemic. Each week, I presented on a particular topic (How to Network Virtually, How to Be a Giver and Be Successful, How to Differentiate Yourself, etc.) with plenty of time for discussion. Interestingly, it was originally supposed to be a four-week series and at the end, it was requested we continue to meet every other week to continue finding sincere ways to assist one another. Every single member of this group became a sincere friend, and every one of these folks would return my calls for sincere reasons. Over time, others joined the group. Many of these people I had not met in person, yet we were all developing real, deep relationships and finding real ways to support one another during the pandemic and after.

We can never have enough of these types of relationships in our lives. However, they do not just happen; we need to make them happen. We cannot afford to wait until we need the relationships (i.e. needing a new job) to develop them. Much like a good salesperson needs to build a consistent sales pipeline, so, too, must we all develop a consistent pipeline of relationships that will serve us well now and for the rest of our lives.

These relationships are often about *loyalty*.

LOYALTY—"A STRONG FEELING OF SUPPORT OR ALLEGIANCE"

Loyalty is an interesting word I am not sure people understand until they are dealing with the ramifications of someone not being loyal. We all probably think we are "loyal" people, but do we really know what this means? Do we know how to put the feeling of being loyal into practice? Over the years, I have realized the true meaning of loyalty is being there for someone when there is nothing in it for you. But how do we know who to be loyal to? Usually, we are loyal to those with whom we have developed past relationships. This only makes sense, and these loyal past relationships can prove unbelievably helpful when the chips are down.

But here's the thing—in order for people to be loyal to you when you need it, you typically need to *prove* loyalty to them first. This is easier said than done. It requires work and faith that the things you do for others to whom you are loyal today may come back to you in the long run—and if they don't, *this must be okay.*

An interesting case study on this idea is the case of the Arthur Andersen accounting firm. The firm was founded in 1913 by Arthur Andersen and Clarence DeLany as Andersen, Delany & Co. The firm changed its name to Arthur Andersen in 1918 and grew to become one of the largest professional services firms in the world. The firm's headquarters were in Chicago, and as someone who lived and worked in Chicago, I had certainly heard of the firm and its storied history. They had a reputation of doing the right thing from an ethical perspective and advising their clients the ethical path was always in their best interest in the long run.

Many of those who joined the firm joined with an expectation of becoming a partner of the firm. The firm was growing like crazy and Chicago was the headquarters. Getting a job at Andersen was a coveted role and getting one of those coveted positions meant you most likely were in for significant success. The firm had a very strong culture, and those who worked at the firm developed their own language, acronyms, and close relationships over time.

When you joined the firm, you were placed in a "start group," which was the group of young folks newly minted out of college who joined the firm on the same day as you. Interestingly, this was at a time when the firm was hiring so many people that every week there would be a new, nicely sized start group. There are many stories of long-term friendships, relationships, and even marriages that started in these start groups.

In 1999, Andersen found itself right in the middle of the largest accounting scandal in the history of the United States. At the time, Andersen was the audit firm for Enron and other publicly traded companies that were found by the US Securities and Exchange Commission to have engaged in significant accounting irregularities. Upon further investigation, it was found that not only were there irregularities, Arthur Andersen & Co. was found guilty of obstructing justice for shredding Enron's financial documents to conceal them from the SEC. This was later overturned on appeal; however, the firm never recovered from this and ended up becoming simply a holding company.[17]

After an investigation, Arthur Andersen and all its approximately eighty-five thousand employees worldwide were put out of business, leaving all of these professionals looking for a next role. Most of these people had never needed to "look for a job," as they had gotten their initial role at Andersen right out of school. Their Arthur Andersen relationships proved to be extremely helpful in many cases.

Over the years, many Arthur Andersen alumni who had ended up leaving the firm ended up in high-level management roles in large companies around the country. With all of this talent hitting the street at one time, it was a competitive time to find a career opportunity.

As I mentioned, the Arthur Andersen culture was tight-knit—and it became even more tight-knit after the Enron scandal. People developed close, sincere professional relationships both internally as well as with their clients. When Arthur Andersen was driven out of business by the Enron scandal,

---

17   Troy Segal, "Enron Scandal: The Fall of a Wall Street Darling," Investopedia, updated January 19th, 2021.

many Andersen alums turned to the folks with whom they grew up in the firm for support—their sincere relationships. While many of these folks had not kept in touch over the years, many of these people offered not only support, but also professional opportunities, as they were in a place to make hiring decisions. It only made sense they would look to manage their risk by hiring folks they had worked with, and whose work with which they were familiar.

This support has become somewhat legendary since the firm went out of business. This dynamic is interesting but not surprising. With so many people displaced at no fault of their own, because these folks had the common experience of starting their careers with Arthur Andersen, the dynamics of alumni status have become very similar to the experiences of being an alum of a particular college, fraternity, or sorority.

Many people who started their careers at Andersen did not actively maintain relationships with those whom they worked with while at the firm. As I mentioned, Andersen alumni would certainly be there for one another; however, the ones who benefited most from this were those who were proactive in maintaining relationships. For many, it wasn't until the firm was put out of business before they realized the importance of maintaining these relationships. However, given their shared pedigree, reaching out was somewhat easy—if one was willing to do so.

One of those who did actively maintain long-term relationships was partner Barry Masek. Barry started his career with Arthur Andersen right out of University of Nebraska—where he grew up on a farm, the oldest of five siblings. As the oldest in his family and having the farm background, he often found himself leading activities with his siblings, and developed leadership skills very early that helped substantially as he moved into his career. As a kid, he played almost every sport and was always surrounded by friends. He was also a pretty smart guy, enjoying anything having to do with computers and numbers. Unlike some who were into these things, Barry also enjoyed developing relationships with others.

Barry was very successful at Arthur Andersen, developing relationships from the day he arrived. He immediately jumped in and got involved with some of the largest, most well-known clients with whom the firm was working at the time.

"I found the best way to get to know the partners above me was to simply do good work. If I did good work and built good relationships, the rest would take care of itself," Barry explained. "I believe in luck and fate and there has been a God looking over me and my family."

As he moved up from not only doing the accounting work to actually selling the work, unlike some, he found this to be an easy transition, given he naturally developed and maintained relationships. Some accountants do not naturally do this—but Barry was not one of them. Barry developed a reputation inside and outside the firm as someone who would give the shirt off his back. He was not looking to make a dollar today; he took a sincere interest in the success of his clients and teams, and it showed.

Barry was so successful at the firm that prior to the firm's fall, one of his clients approached him to join their company as their CFO. This was a difficult decision for anyone to make, and Barry made the decision to leave the firm and join his client. Therefore, Barry was able to avoid the fall of the firm.

"Sometimes it is better to be lucky than smart, but seriously, it was the right time for me to take a CFO role," Barry said.

After spending six years as CFO of a large distribution company in Chicago, Barry left to find his next CFO opportunity. Andersen was gone and his former partners, who were now at Big 4 firms, were unhappy and dismayed the public accounting world had changed. Barry was not planning on getting back into public accounting. However, in his search process, he met a small, growing accounting firm based in Wisconsin called Baker Tilly that had just merged with a small firm based in Chicago and decided to join the firm. Baker Tilly realized Barry had a unique skill set, in that he was technical and someone who understood how to grow sincere relationships with clients as well as his internal teams. I had an opportunity to work with Barry for eight years at Baker Tilly and experience this up close. It was truly something to see.

Given the culture of Arthur Andersen—it is almost as if you fought in the same war and were in the same foxhole when you find a fellow Andersen alum—there is an automatic bond that is comparable to attending the same college or being in the same fraternity.

As we make buying decisions, we all like to work with people we can sincerely trust, and we look for points of commonality when making important decisions. Given the number of people who were impacted by the fall of Andersen, if you are alumni of Andersen, you have a baked-in network of others in the marketplace.

Since joining Baker Tilly, many of Barry's clients have been his former Arthur Andersen clients and associates.

STAY IN TOUCH WITH THOSE YOU WORK WITH!

"Barry, can you be here tomorrow? I have a situation I need your help with."

This was the call Barry received while at Baker Tilly from a fellow Arthur Andersen alum with whom Barry had worked. The call came the day after this alum took a role as CFO of a company that was in the midst of substantial accounting issues. He needed an accounting firm to assist with digging out of the issues—a major project, and one where this CFO needed to feel he was able to completely trust whatever firm he decided to partner with. This was more than deciding on a firm to work with. The decision would determine in large part whether this CFO would be successful in his role. He needed to bring someone in who he sincerely trusted.

Barry went to meet with his friend and from the moment he arrived, it was clear the work was his. The sincere trust had already been established over many years, starting when they worked together at Andersen. Barry is an excellent accountant; *however, this is not why his firm was hired.* His firm was hired because he was personally and sincerely trusted to partner with his friend and ensure the work was done well.

People often do not hire the smartest person or firm—they hire the smartest person or firm *they can trust*.

There are literally hundreds of stories just like this one that are clear examples of the benefits of the sincere, long-term relationships that were developed at Arthur Andersen, and the loyalty those who worked at the firm have to one another.

This type of loyalty can make one's professional life easier, as it is easier to do business when you are trusted. It also impacts one's personal life for so many reasons. If you have great relationships, you will have more job security, better friendships, and more security in maintaining client relationships. All of these things will improve your quality of life and make your life more fulfilling!

This type of loyalty can be started with clients, teammates on sports teams, etc., and can lead to great professional gain. But it can also lead to incredible personal gain. *This approach will impact your entire life.*

Arthur Andersen is a great example of a moment in time where a leading global entity disappeared almost overnight. Those who worked there share something in common others do not share, and they have proven to be unbelievably supportive to one another. History has shown people benefit from having a network of people who support them, or better yet, multiple networks. The Arthur Andersen network is extremely strong and supportive, and those who are lucky enough to be a part of it have, like Barry Masek, had a much easier time finding clients and professional opportunities.

If everyone can find a solid network of folks with whom they have things in common—and work hard to develop sincere relationships with people in this network—these stories prove life gets easier and more rewarding in the long run, and incredibly satisfying as well!

In a later chapter, I will provide a framework for developing unbelievable and truly life-changing relationships throughout your life. I will provide additional real-world examples of people who have been wildly successful in large part due to their sincere network and the way it continues to build. I will also provide examples of companies and entities that have proven to have sincere cultures in terms of the way they do business, take care of their people, clients, and customers, and the overall experience of working with these companies.

CHAPTER 5

The Work-Life Balance Mistake—Creating "Work-Life Integration"

———

Have you ever had a goal you badly wanted to attain but you had absolutely no idea how to make it happen? We have all been through this. It might be a personal goal around health or fitness, or it might be a professional goal to take your career in a different direction. In order to accomplish these goals, one needs to take proactive steps and often connect with the right people.

In 2013, I received an unexpected call from a friend. Our relationship had started approximately ten years prior when I cold-called him and he became my client. He had two children from a prior marriage and had recently gotten remarried; he and his wife were expecting a daughter. This is what he said:

"Aaron, my wife and I have so much respect for you and Lisa and how you have raised your kids. Our families are both not in the United States, and we were wondering if you would be willing to be in our will to take care of our daughter should something happen to us?"

After tearing up and pulling over my car to get my wits about me, I wondered how over 10 years a relationship could evolve from a cold-call to being asked to parent someone's child? After all, this was not the only such relationship I had developed in my life and my career, but I realized at that moment it was not only about the quantity of conversations or relationships I had developed over my life and career. There was a mutually beneficial, sincere quality to this relationship as well as many of my other relationships that could not be faked.

The common advice people receive is to maintain a "work-life balance" in order to ensure they do not overwork, they spend enough time with their family and friends, and they set up boundaries to make sure their most important relationships get the time they deserve and need. Critics of the term "work-life balance" say those who strive to live this lifestyle create "an artificial separation between work and life, as if work were not a part of life. Others say it incorrectly implies a zero-sum equation in which life loses out while you're working, and vice versa."[18]

The result of this is people do not realize they are inadvertently creating a barrier to sincere relationships due to the

---

18 Dorcas, Cheng-Tozum, "Work-Life Balance vs. Work-Life Integration: How Are They Different and Which One Is For You?" *Inc.com*, March 14, 2018.

behavior this desire to keep a "balance" between work and life creates.

There is another paradigm to consider. I have found the most successful, content, and generally happy people I have gotten to know throughout my career employ more of a "work-life integration" approach to relationships. They do not put up artificial boundaries around what they discuss, how they discuss it, etc. They will discuss personal things about their families openly, they will humbly ask for help or advice, and they simply act *like a friend* from the beginning of the relationship. This approach has been talked about more and more in recent years, and according to the University of California Berkeley's Haas School of Business, work-life integration is "an approach that creates more synergies between all areas that define 'life': work, home/family, community, personal well-being, and health."[19]

None of the people I write about in this book really do work-life balance in the way most people think about. They use this "work-life integration" approach naturally where the relationships they develop professionally are not kept separate from their personal relationships - rather they are naturally integrated. This is a delicate balance, and in Chapter Six, I will lay out the framework you can use to both get comfortable with work-life integration and how to accomplish it throughout your life and career.

This "work-life integration" approach to relationships can be life-changing. You do not need to do this naturally; however,

---

19   Ibid.

finding ways to work this approach into relationships in your life will undoubtedly make your life more fulfilling. Just like not needing to be an extrovert to be successful, I highly suggest trying to approach your professional relationships like friendships—you will be amazed at how things will change.

If you nurture sincere relationships and stay focused on your goals, anything is possible!

During the process of writing this book, I had an opportunity to be involved in a group discussion with Mario Armstrong, who shared many of the stories below. After that, I talked with Mario a couple of times directly and I can tell you he is a tremendous human being. His success is not surprising. He is a person who always had extremely high aspirations. As a young man growing up in Maryland, Mario badly wanted a career in television or radio; however, he did not have any practical, real-world experience. He sincerely wanted to take his career in a progressive direction, and come hell or high water, he was going to make it happen. In meeting Mario, one thing was clear: this is a man who accomplishes his goals and doesn't rest until he makes them happen.

Mario went to college for communications; however, due to some crazy turn of events in college, he did not graduate with an undergraduate degree. In some ways, that might have made Mario hungrier, but regardless of the situation, Mario planned to accomplish his goals.

Rather than doing what many do when they do not graduate college—which is to settle for something less than their original goal—Mario stayed true to his goal and forged ahead.

He had tunnel vision to figure something out in the area about which he was passionate and went to school—television or radio.

Mario found a small AM radio station in Annapolis, Maryland, that was selling thirty-minutes of airtime every Thursday. Fortunately, at the time, Mario only worked fifteen minutes away. So, every Thursday for three years, he would leave his job at noon, make the fifteen-minute commute, do a thirty-minute show for free, and drive the fifteen minutes back to work. The entire time he did this, he was building the relationships and portfolio of work that would allow him to find unbelievable success later in his life and his career. Keep in mind, he did this as his side hustle while still keeping his full-time job—he sincerely wanted to accomplish his goals!

"I was convinced I was going to work in this industry, and I found this small AM radio station in Annapolis, Maryland. You could throw a stone down the street and that was quite possibly as far as I could be heard," Mario explained. "The studio was in an old farmhouse with a small satellite in the back, and even though I had never done a radio show before, it was a start."

What Mario clearly knew back then, and what I have been known to say as I look to assist people in implementing the ideas outlined in this book:

"You don't fail when you try—you learn when you try."

Now that Mario had an AM radio demo, he realized he could get to a larger FM audience. FM stations knew he had been successful on AM radio. He had a demo to show them he was serious and had talent and he had a great story to tell as he looked for these FM radio jobs.

After getting an FM gig and moving to NPR Radio as their tech contributor—both as a side hustle while still maintaining a full-time job—Mario was ready to conquer the next goal of getting to television. However, at that time this was not so easy—so he used the sincere relationships he had built to approach TV stations and say, "Take a look at what I have done on radio. I would like to come on your show one morning per week and do a technology segment." One of his longtime relationships agreed to give him a half hour once a week.

Not only would Mario show up every single week for three years, he would show up with donuts and coffee and walk around getting to know people at all levels. Mario showed very clearly that humility and simply being a nice person are extremely important parts of being genuine.

When Mario meets people, he is immediately thinking and asking questions about what the other person is trying to accomplish and is looking to bring sincere value to the other person. After all, this is how pure and authentic relationships evolve.

"Most people do not understand the power they have when coming into a new relationship, or in managing the relationships they already have," explains Mario. "People do not understand the power of leverage. They give others way too much power and don't realize that by bringing sincere value, they are able to seize some of that power back and use it for the benefit of both sides of the relationship. It is extremely powerful."

The most important thing is to be sincere about what you do for others. Mario did not show up with donuts and coffee for any other reason than he wanted to be a nice guy—it is just who he is—and guess what? People took him as he intended. He asked a ton of questions and realized those around him who had accomplished the things he wanted to accomplish were just as eager to answer his questions as he was to ask them. He searched for mentors successfully. These people passionately helped Mario accomplish his goals and vice versa. This has been Mario's secret for success. Although Mario has attained amazing success, he still takes the time to mentor young folks, as it is tremendously gratifying.

The most sincerely giving people are the most successful over time.

Mario had attained a measure of success, but that was not enough for him; in fact, it only fueled him to want to do more and attain more goals. Rather than settling and waiting for the phone to ring with new opportunities, he went and made it happen. In order to do that, he needed to take additional risk, connect with more people, build more relationships, and lead with purely giving first without looking for an immediate return. He realized he needed to bring sincere value to every relationship, and if he stayed true to this mission and calling, he would accomplish all of his goals, dreams, and more.

"Too many people wait for opportunities and people to find them rather than going and finding it themselves," says

Mario. "We now live in a world where you don't have to wait. If you want a job building websites, don't wait to get hired building websites. Build a couple of websites to begin a portfolio to give people a reason to believe you can bring them sincere value. Those who live their lives in this way tend to be the most successful."

In order to really make this all possible in the long term, the approach to work-life integration is much easier to accomplish when you are doing something you are passionate about. Finding others who are passionate about the same things makes it that much easier, and you will never feel like your life is out of balance.

As I mentioned, I met Mario through the process of writing this book when he joined one of our book writing sessions. Although he has attained incredible levels of success, he offered to meet with anyone in the group to discuss their book concept or anything else they might want to discuss—and he meant it.

THE ART OF WORK-LIFE INTEGRATION

As I speak with people about this concept, I find at first, people are skeptical. They want to have uninterrupted family time and time with their friends. Work-life integration is actually the opposite of this—it gives you the opportunity to create more pure and authentic friendships throughout your life with people who can add value to your life in all sorts of ways.

On the professional side of our lives, companies and entities do not hire people or create business deals with other companies or entities—real, living people do these things. The more people we know and the more sincere relationships we develop, the easier it is to find business opportunities, and the more fulfilled our lives become.

Mario has accomplished many of his goals and he is still not done. He has launched a new season of the *Never Settle Show*, a new course to teach you how to access brand sponsorships to fund your ideas. He regularly appears as a digital lifestyle expert on *The Today Show* and NPR. Recently, he has partnered with Daymond John of *Shark Tank*. He has also won two Emmy Awards for his show *Never Settle*—Best Interactivity and Best Program Host in 2018, and numerous other awards.[20]

However, given his success, this has only further fueled Mario's desire to sincerely help others accomplish their goals. He often spends time mentoring college students and young aspiring entrepreneurs. He is a living example of what is possible when you live this type of sincere lifestyle.

Another example of someone who does not separate relationships is Benny Mathew.

Benny is lucky to be alive.

The date was October 8, 2000, and he was headed back to Northern Illinois University where he was a freshman in college. He didn't have a care in the world, was with his

---

20   "Mario Armstrong: Motivating People around the World to Never Settle," Marioarmstrong.com, accessed January 30, 2021.

best friends, and was doing what countless young people do every single day.

Suddenly out of nowhere—bam! The SUV in which Benny and his friends were riding was slammed into, and Benny was knocked unconscious. He needed to be extricated from the vehicle and was in terrible shape; he almost died. Suddenly, Benny found himself on a ventilator for over two months; two months of which he has no recollection. He shattered one of his hips, broke the other, his ribs were fractured, his lungs collapsed, he broke his wrist and seven fingers, he had a basial skull fracture which caused brain fluid to leak from his left ear, and the left side of his face was temporarily paralyzed. Because of the brain fluid leaking, he lost 100 percent of his hearing in his left ear.

Every day, Benny's mom, dad, brother, sister, coworkers, and best friends would hold a vigil at his bedside. Benny was a guy who was loved by everyone who knew him, and in his time of need, people showed up to support him and his family.

"I knew I had great relationships," explains Benny. "But I had no idea people would show up for me in the way they did. It further showed me the power of what relationships can become with people, even when they are not blood-related."

Everyone showed up for Benny from every part of his life, past and present. Although he was only a freshman in college and was not working in a professional role, Benny was already not separating the relationships in his life. Benny was simply a guy who was so genuine that when the chips were down, people were there for him. As you will see, these behaviors were the root of the behaviors that have driven the professional relationships that have made Benny successful.

Prior to this unfortunate accident, Benny was always someone who was driven by relationships. He and his family moved to the suburbs of Chicago when he was seven years old in 1989. At the time, he spoke virtually no English and his family had very little money. They were moving there to create a better life for themselves.

They moved into a very small apartment in Melrose Park, Illinois.

"When I moved here, it was difficult as a kid in a new world where I did not speak the language. I lived in a tiny apartment. I wanted to build relationships and get to know people. This has been embedded in me forever. Therefore, I started playing basketball and getting involved in rap music in school to get to know people, connect with people, and build relationships," explains Benny.

Interestingly, Benny explained at this point in his life, he realized he had an authentic desire to meet new people and get to know them. He realized if you take a sincere interest in other people and stay consistent in building relationships, great things happen—he also genuinely enjoyed getting to know people. Carrying this belief into his life led him to build a strong network of relationships before he was even in need of professional connections.

After his life-changing accident, Benny returned to school with a renewed appreciation for the types of authentic relationships he had already developed with others. He began to find himself being a connector for others, and he truly enjoyed helping others accomplish whatever they tried to accomplish. He never felt a need to ask for anything in return. He was just someone who enjoyed making other people's lives better and doing so sincerely.

Upon finishing college in 2004, Benny went into the staffing business in the suburbs of Chicago, a business that has a reputation for being extremely transactional. In fact, the American Staffing Association finds the median annual turnover rate in the staffing industry is 25 percent, which means that one out of every four employees are leaving their staffing firm each year. Most people who start in the industry are simply not successful, and those who are successful in the long run are successful due in large part to the relationships they develop.[21]

Over the years, the staffing industry has become extremely commoditized. It used to be that recruiters and staffing professionals were required to build deep relationships with people in the marketplace. Companies would develop their own proprietary databases of contacts, and these databases would grow as the relationships of those who worked at the firm grew.

Today, everyone has access to LinkedIn and other websites, and in many ways, everyone has access to the same information. If we want to find someone, all we need to do is go to LinkedIn or Google, insert their name, and a world of information is at our fingertips. This can be seen as a good thing;

---

21   Eric Gregg, "The Cost of Internal Employee Turnover in Staffing," *Clearly Rated (blog)*, December 12, 2019.

however, does it help us start and build new relationships and maintain old ones? Given that this amount of information is out there on all of us, how do we differentiate ourselves personally and professionally so people will know we are truly sincere and not like everyone else they meet?

These things are more important than ever. Creating great relationships will help us capitalize on the information we are able to find on others and that is available about us, and eventually to differentiate ourselves from others.

In the staffing business, you are taught to sell. You cold-call, you are expected to generate a significant amount of activity, and it needs to be done while being perceived as sincere. Benny did all he was asked and trained to do, and he took it to the extreme.

In fact, Benny did not know when to take "no" for an answer, which was a good thing for two reasons. The first reason was there was no way he would have been successful had he not been diligent. The second reason was Benny is just a likable guy. Once you meet him, his sincerity truly oozes through the fiber of his being—it cannot be faked. Interestingly, this can be said for all of those I interviewed for this book; but again, it is something everyone is capable of, as most are already doing these things in their personal lives.

Intent on doing business with a particular company, Benny called the HR manager, Sally, numerous times with no success. As Benny was known to do, and as someone who did not take "no" for an answer, Benny called the other hiring managers at the company and met with any of them who were willing to meet. When they met, he opened up personally, offered to assist in any way he could personally or professionally, and always kept every single promise, even when he was not being paid to do so.

Each of these hiring managers referred him back to Sally, and finally, Benny found himself in a meeting with her. As they talked about their lives, families, and careers and got to know one another, Benny did not push for business. At the time, Sally was somewhat content with another provider who was a bit less expensive. Benny was unperturbed by this, as Sally was clearly the type of *person* with whom he wanted to do business and know now and into the future.

A couple of weeks later, Benny got a call from Sally with an opportunity to fill a small role, something to give him an opportunity to show Sally and the company what he could do when given the opportunity. He knocked it out of the park, got a next opportunity, and blew that one away as well! A couple of months later, he became their exclusive provider. Benny has many of these stories from throughout his career and life, and as you talk with him, it is very clear he truly appreciates the fact he is still here to make this sincere difference in other people's lives.

In 2017, Benny joined me at Baker Tilly to run the staffing division, giving him a larger suite of solutions to serve his network. This was the first time Benny had worked in downtown Chicago, and he found it very difficult to get in front of prospects. It was a tough first year.

I brought him to networking events and introduced him to executives around the Chicago market, showing him how to ensure these folks successfully met others in the market-place who would help them be successful over time. I helped him understand the concept and value of being a "center of influence," how that allowed you to purely and sincerely help others and gave you access to these folks when you want to discuss business opportunities. To be honest, Benny was such a natural I really didn't have to do much.

Being the smart guy that Benny is, he saw an opportunity. Benny realized the majority of today's professionals across all industries and at all levels truly had no idea how to net-work. The word was overused and under-defined. Much like I realized, Benny realized if he helped people with the frame-work of building sincere, mutually beneficial relationships, he would most likely never have to cold-call again.

Rather than simply creating one-on-one introductions, in 2018, Benny created the *Orion3 Networking Group*. His idea was based on the 'Power of 3' and is basically a network of profes-sionals, in Chicago at all levels, that is dedicated to sincerely helping others accomplish their personal and professional hopes and dreams. Through *Orion3*. Benny has met count-less people he can call friends. More importantly, it is because of Benny that literally hundreds of people know one another.

The value of your network is not the num-ber of people you know—*it is the num-ber of people who know one another as a result of your efforts that matters!*

In February 2021, in the middle of the COVID-19 pandemic, Benny was able to make the ultimate decision. Due to the amazing relationships he had developed with professionals in Chicago, as well as the corporate sponsors who had sponsored *Orion3* since its founding, Benny decided to leave Baker Tilly to make this passion project his full-time job. Had it not been for the amazing relationships he developed, this would have never been possible!

Benny went from someone who, in 2000, almost lost his life in a devastating accident to truly impacting, inspiring, and changing the lives of numerous others for the better over the years. Every single day, people meet one another as a result of Benny's efforts—and he has created tremendous relationships for himself as a result!

All of this goes to show if we are open to being vulnerable with those we meet, open up about our goals, discuss our families, and simply let people in by eliminating the artificial barriers we often put up in professional relationships, we will build better relationships and live more fulfilled lives. In the next chapter, I will discuss specific steps you can take to begin living this life. If we live this type of life, the people we meet might truly change our lives!

CHAPTER 6

General Framework for Building Sincere Relationships

——

It is very difficult to be successful in doing something without a good framework to follow. Building new relationships and connecting is no different. One of the reasons I felt the need to write this book is the frustration of hearing "experts" expressing the importance of "networking" without explaining *how to actually do it,* the actual framework of being a successful networker and living a sincere life.

If you have gotten this far in this book, you now believe sincere relationships are an important part of living one's best possible life. What next? These days, the formula to creating great relationships often takes the form of some sort of "networking." Over the past several years, networking has taken on a life of its own, with people realizing it is simply a necessary part of most professional careers. However, what really differentiates the successful from the non-successful networkers? What makes people great relationship builders?

The answer has become crystal clear to me—sincerity in every single interaction.

WHAT DOES NETWORKING REALLY MEAN?

The challenge is that the word "networking" is an overused and under-defined term.

A couple of years ago I was attending the Spring Luncheon for the University of Illinois College of Business in Chicago. This event takes place every spring, and all the "movers and shakers" of Chicago business tend to show up. That year, the CFO of the Allstate Insurance Company, for whom I had worked years before when I did an internship at Allstate while getting my MBA, was being honored. I knew this meant his entire family would most likely be there. Over the years since working for him, I had stayed in loose touch with him, reaching out to say hello every year.

My goal was to reconnect with him, congratulate him, and hopefully create a situation where I could set up lunch to discuss mutually beneficial business opportunities, of which there were many. He greeted me very warmly, introduced me to his wife and son, and we briefly discussed who I should meet with on his team. It was a testament to the importance of keeping in touch and how doing so sincerely can give you access to leaders of major companies to discuss mutually beneficial opportunities.

At the beginning of the event, I saw two of my younger associates from my firm and I mentioned the CFO of Allstate was being honored and I had a strategy, a sincere strategy to use this networking event to further professional goals. Both of them looked at me as if a light bulb had gone off and they realized this wasn't just a chance for a nice lunch—it was an opportunity to begin or further relationships that could advance our professional goals. They had not learned to do this in the past, and from here, they mentioned they planned to approach these types of events differently in the future!

The words "networking," "pay it forward," "be a giver," and others like those have become buzzwords and almost taken on a negative connotation, as most people are simply not sincere when going about their networking journey. Most people approach it with their hand out or wait until they *need* to network in order to get a job, sell something, or accomplish another transaction. This is not the best way to create long-term relationships and get the most out of your networking journey.

When I first set out to write this book, I thought I was simply writing a book about networking. As I interviewed those who have been most successful and considered my own life, I realized we all have one thing in common—sincerity in most everything we do. The question becomes how to ensure sincerity is taken as intended and one is not lumped in with all of the others who think they are sincere but do not really understand the meaning of the word.

In his book *Start with Why,* Simon Sinek talks about how *why* you are doing something is actually more important in the long run than *what* you are doing. This is particularly the case in building relationships. As you think about your own life, none of us want to build relationships with people who solely wish to get to know us for some sort of selfish reason, be it in business or personal relationships. When we meet people through friends and those we know well, there is almost an immediate sense of trust, particularly as compared to meeting people independent of a common connection. If we perceive the other party's "why" is a selfish one, we will either not take the relationship to the next level or we will proceed with extreme caution that might either delay or entirely stop any potential progress in the relationship.[22]

THE FORMULA FOR GIVERS

In order to be perceived as sincere, you need to be sincere—there is no faking it.

The formula of being a Giver while still being increasingly personally and professionally successful and fulfilled throughout one's life is somewhat simple. Many who write and speak about professional networking tout a process, which I am hesitant to do. We all develop relationships in different ways, and what works for my personality might not work for yours. Rather, I present this as a *framework* to consider, depending on where you are in your career, along with a few action steps you can consistently make on your own. You must make this your own—again, realize you do

---

22   Simon Sinek. *Start with Why: How Great Leaders Inspire Action* (New York: Penguin Publishing Group, 2009).

not have to be an extrovert; however, you need to be comfortable getting to know new people.

The good news is, regardless of where you find yourself in your career, there are aspects of this framework that can be applied today to get you almost immediate results. These results will be measured in more relationships. First, a few things to consider:

- People hire people, and they make decisions about which firms they hire and who they work with. Therefore, we all need to meet more people.
- People make decisions related to those with whom they develop personal relationships, and the best personal relationships we develop throughout our lives will be with people we meet through other people.

Therefore, logic dictates we all need to meet, get to know, and foster real relationships throughout our lives. Before LinkedIn, Facebook, Twitter, and social media in general, it was more imperative people met one another. In order to do business with a bank, you needed to go to the bank. In order to buy insurance, you needed to talk with a human. In order to buy products, you needed to go to a store. If you wanted to meet another human to get to know, date, etc., you had to actually meet them. Now, all you need to do is log in. This has created a huge opportunity for those who wish to seize it—the opportunity to build real, authentic relationships!

Most people think of large networking events with hundreds of people, tables of ten, cocktail hours, etc. Some people do quite well in this setting while most people attend these types of events with very little to show for it after attending.

Therefore, I have realized the magic happens through what I call *"micro-networking."* Micro-networking is when one person meets another, gets an understanding of what they are trying to accomplish personally or professionally, and proactively makes introductions that will help both people accomplish their collective goals. By doing this, you are becoming a "Center of Influence," and Centers of Influence always have their calls returned.

ALWAYS BE A CENTER OF INFLUENCE

A "Center of Influence" is someone who is well-known, respected, and trusted in the community by their peers or in their industry and, as a result, has significant influence over the thoughts and actions of others. We all want to become a Center of Influence, and depending on the level in your career, the roadmap to getting there is different.

Contrary to many people's opinions, it is unnecessary to be in sales to become a Center of Influence. In fact, those who become most successful over time are Centers of Influence in either their industry, community, company, and in life in general.

Their mind-set tends to be more broad, holistic, and strategic. They think outside the box, and they are very comfortable sharing their informed opinion.

Therefore, you always want to be the one proactively thinking about who others need to know in your network, and you want to proactively make these introductions. Regardless of the level you are at in your career, this will set you apart.

I want to emphasize we all need to become Centers of Influence in the world we live in, both in the communities in which we live as well as the industries in which we work. The more people we know in our industry, and more importantly, the more people who know us, the easier it will be to meet the people we want to meet throughout our lives.

So what does this all mean? It means that, like anything else, to be successful, you need to utilize a framework that you make your own. I have provided specific suggestions below depending on where you find yourself in your career and life, but it is important you make this your own. Make sure you allow yourself to be genuine and sincere as you do these things. Most importantly, do not be afraid to step out of your comfort zone. Much of this will take being a bit bold at first and possibly stepping outside of your comfort zone, but as you see success in the results of the sincere relationships you develop as a result of these behaviors, your life will improve incredibly as a result.

COLLEGE AND EARLY STAGE CAREER
This is an ideal time to build the network you will need for the rest of your career. For those who really do this well and sincerely, it actually starts in high school and college.

However, as I have spoken with and mentored people at this stage in their careers, they are often hesitant to jump into the deep end and integrate their personal and professional relationships. This is due to many things: the people they see around them at work who are not sincere, the examples their parents have set as they lived their lives, and other things they have been exposed to. This creates a hesitancy that, to be honest, will hold those with the most potential back from accomplishing the most they can over the course of their life. Those who are bold can often accomplish more than those who get the best grades and are considered "book smart."

In college, one should not just go to a good school and attend class. It is more important than ever before to get involved on campus and become a connector for others as early in your college career as possible—possibly as early as high school. Find mentors early. The best Centers of Influence later in their careers are those who make the most connections for others, and this should start as early as possible.

Once you have landed your first professional role, it is important to continue staying in touch with people you went to college with and have worked with, particularly those who work in roles that are peripheral to your industry. Many people think being connected on LinkedIn is enough, but it isn't. Here are my suggestions:

- Develop a list of your college and childhood friends who are smart, have taken great entry-level roles, and are people you enjoy and would like to keep in touch with.
- Reach out proactively and let them know your intent to keep in touch as you move throughout your careers. Offer to facilitate introductions over time and deliver on them. Build relationships.

- Deliver on your promises. The key to sincerity is following through. There are many people who talk a good game but do not follow through on their promises. Commit to being a connector throughout your career. Follow through on this consistently and your life and career will become much more interesting and fulfilling.
- Create a database of contacts you store on your local computer or that you have personal access to. Do not allow your contacts to only be stored on your company devices.
- Send out well-written update e-mails and follow up on them. When possible, make them personal to each individual. This will allow you to use these as a way to advance your relationships. There are many programs such as Constant Contact and Mixmax that make these communications easy.
- In Chapter Eight, I tell the story of my friend Allan Loeb, an extremely successful screenwriter in Hollywood (*Wall Street: Money Never Sleeps*, *The Switch*, *Rock of Ages*, *The Only Living Boy in New York*, etc.) He gives specific suggestions for how to run meetings with new contacts. The suggestions can and should be utilized in any networking meeting you have if you are looking to bring these relationships to the next level. Allan applied this advice himself to build the relationships that have helped fuel his success.

One of my favorite sayings is "you can't boil the ocean." This concept applied here is to take a couple of your closer relationships and just try it. Put it out there, find a couple of people in your network who need to know one another and introduce them. You will be absolutely amazed by what happens!

In Adam Grant's book *Give and Take,* he talks about the Five-Minute Favor, which basically says any favor that takes five minutes or less is a favor we should be willing to do for others at any time. This is an amazing concept to keep in mind. If possible, try to create introductions for others every single week, possibly multiple times per week. Make sure they are sincere, but like many other things in life, you will get out of this what you put into it.[23]

Make sure people realize you are looking for mutually beneficial relationships. Be an evangelist for the importance of relationships.

I will often ask those who are uncomfortable with this the following question: If I were to send you a well-written introduction to another interesting person, would you appreciate it? Guess what, everyone says yes, but few people do this, and that is your real opportunity.

A perfect example of someone who has done this throughout her life is Paige Arnof-Fenn.

"I don't collect things, I collect people—and I always have."
PAIGE ARNOF-FENN

Paige has always been a people person. Even as a young kid, she was always wired. She knew everyone. She never needed to try to make friends—quite the contrary, Paige is everyone's friend. Once you have met her, you have an opportunity to

---

23   Adam Grant. *Give and Take* (New York, Penguin USA, 2013).

become her friend. However, this does not happen automatically. In order to build a relationship with Paige, you need to invest the time to actually build a mutually beneficial relationship—a friendship. Unfortunately, when most people think of "networking," they are thinking of doing so for a very specific purpose.

"I don't think of myself as a networker," she says. "I think of myself as a people person who really enjoys building meaningful, real, and sincere relationships."

In my experience, as well as from the discussions I had with the amazing "networkers" I interviewed for this book, people like Paige network naturally as a result of the way they live their lives. They are genuine, authentic, and real people, but these people realize you need to do the work in the relationship in order to reap the rewards. This takes sincere giving without expecting anything in return. Paige has been this person her whole life.

Paige spent the beginning part of her career in marketing roles with companies such as Procter & Gamble and Coca-Cola. She worked on marketing the 1996 Olympics and spent time as the top marketing professional at three successful start-ups—all of which had successful exits. Paige and her husband moved to Boston in 1999, where they planned to stay for a short time. Twenty-one years later, they are still happily living in the Boston area.

Upon moving, Paige immediately joined two professional women's groups to get to know other professionals in Boston. Unlike many people who would go to events to "network,"

Paige never thought of it this way. Interestingly, the best networkers do not think of it as overtly networking. Paige was intent on meeting people and doing what she had always done—building sincere and real relationships that could and would grow over time.

Paige attended Stanford for her undergraduate degree, and most people know Stanford is a very entrepreneurial environment. Many Stanford graduates have gone on to create and do great things. One of Paige's very good friends was the co-founder of LinkedIn. When he and his team were developing the site, he would joke with her that she was his muse. You see, Paige was one of the first people he knew who would consistently create "e-introductions" for those in her network. These would sometimes be requested, and other times, they were people who she simply knew well enough to realize they would benefit from knowing one another.

She always makes these introductions personal and sincere. She has a reason for making the introduction she has thought through—Paige realizes this is a huge opportunity to further develop sincere relationships! She does not simply make superficial introductions through LinkedIn or other means.

As I said earlier, as is the case with many things, it is not what you do, but how you do it that counts. Unlike many others, when Paige creates an introduction between two people in her network, she takes the time to write a well-written, personalized introduction not just introducing, but including *why* she is making the introduction. She realizes this is a chance to create another sincere building block toward the structure of a real relationship.

Although Paige and I had never discussed this prior to meeting, interestingly, we had this completely in common!

The fact is no one likes to be sold to— however, people are always open to buying well from those they know, trust, and with whom they have a real relationship.

Through the sincere and real relationships Paige has built over many years, she has become what she calls the "accidental entrepreneur." In late 2001, Paige founded Mavens & Moguls, which in many ways is the culmination of decades of networking without realizing it was networking. She has created a network of seasoned marketing experts around the globe, and she will bring in the professionals with the appropriate experience to create value in cooperation with each client. It is truly a natural extension of how Paige lives her life.

Interestingly, although Paige is a classically trained marketer, she does not really market her company—she doesn't have to; it is all done through word of mouth and relationships. She is a constant, consistent figure at professional events in Boston where she knows many, many people, and this has truly been the lifeblood for the growth of her company.

Paige sees networking and marketing as much the same thing, the two being difficult to disconnect. She once had a professor who said marketing is everything and everything is marketing. She feels strongly that we all represent our own brand, and we need to understand what that brand stands for. If one is not interesting and does not stand out from the pack, people will not want to talk to them, just like a brand.

Growing up in the South gave her an education. "Ultimately, we do business with people—and often the more you chase people, the more they move away."

"Manners matter," Paige says. "My mother sent me to etiquette school. She expected me to say please and thank you. The South is social, so you talk to people—I have no fear of talking to anyone. I love to find interesting people and look for common ground. I think of every encounter as a potential connection, and if I am genuinely interested in what they are doing, then a real connection will be formed." It is truly simple.

A few years ago, Paige wrote a short article titled "Manners Matter" and sent it to some folks in her network. It was very well-received and found its way to the Dean at the Sloan Business School at MIT. She received a call from the dean with a request to include the article in the welcome package at orientation. "Paige, your article could not be more spot-on. The young people who enter this program often do not understand the importance of manners and how you treat others," he said.

Interestingly, I read an article about Paige and reached out to her on LinkedIn to request an interview for this book. I did not necessarily expect a response—certainly not as quickly as I received one.

"Aaron, it is great to meet you! The first thing I want to say is I typically do not accept blind LinkedIn requests."

This was the first thing Paige said when we talked. Of course, I asked her, "Why did you respond to my request? What was different about it?"

She was excited to have the conversation since I did not ask for anything other than an interview and to possibly include her in a book, which anyone might certainly appreciate! I did not write, "We went to the same college so we should get to know one another." I did not write, "We both work in marketing," "We both went to Stanford" (which I didn't), and I did not try to sell anything.

I simply said she had an interesting background, I was writing a book on the best relationship builders in the country, and I may want to include her inspiring story in my book. She got back to me in twenty minutes.

The moral of all of this is to always be connecting but avoid the temptation of trying to generate an immediate transaction of some sort. Look to meet interesting people who share common interests and values and write sincere e-introductions. Listen to people to understand their goals, both personal as well as professional, and help people achieve them. Invite people to join you for personal and professional activities. Much like my friend Paige, this approach will change your life, the lives of others, and ultimately may create truly life-changing opportunities now and over time.

MID-CAREER

At this point in one's career, they have often allowed inertia to take them to different roles. They often found their initial role out of college or graduate school through a recruiter or placement office, and they possibly have progressed internally inside a company or left that original company due to being recruited out by another company for a role at either the next level or for more money.

Tools like LinkedIn that basically allow all professionals to advertise their own personal brand will sometimes create new career opportunities that lead to new relationships. However, these are transactions; the point of these things is not to help you build relationships. The goal, or the "why," of a typical recruiter is to fill a role for their client so they can get paid. Therefore, I suggest taking more control of the proactive relationships you develop over time and work to become a Center of Influence.

Here are a couple of suggestions for those who have reached that midpoint in their career where they are starting to develop an area of specialty in a particular industry or role:

- Go through your contacts on LinkedIn, Facebook, etc., and consider—is this a "contact" for me or someone with whom I have a real relationship? One of the best ways to tell this is to ask yourself, "Would this person return my call?" As you look through these contacts, both personal and professional, consider which of these are people who are doing interesting things about which you have a sincere desire to learn, as well as which complement the direction you have gone in your career. Many people use LinkedIn to professionally network, and they try to collect as many connections as possible. These connections are simply not helpful. The goal is to turn them into real relationships.

- Many people separate their network into personal and professional relationships. As discussed earlier, do not do that. Consider these people to be personal relationships and treat them as such. If you identify sincere ways of adding value to people's careers and lives, they will appreciate it and it will come back to you over and over again.

- Be a connector and hold yourself accountable. Let people know of your intent to connect them to others and why you have found it to be so important. Be an evangelist and inspire people; it will go a long way.

- Identify professional organizations that align with your professional and personal interests and get involved. Don't simply attend meetings; use these meetings as opportunities to collect new relationships and connect people proactively. Become a leader, join committees, and differentiate yourself within the group.

- You should hold yourself accountable for creating a certain number of proactive introductions for others over time. As I have mentioned, many people only start to "network" when they are in transition or think something might be about to take place. This is too late. You must micro-network and build real relationships consistently and with discipline to see results, and you must be sincere while doing so, as people will see right through it if you are not.

- Consider creating a relationship/introductions group for your peers, where you can bring people together to discuss different relevant topics on a regular basis. If you are the one who brings people together and encourages them to get to know one another as well, they will talk positively about you with others and your reputation will grow. This will automatically make you into a Center of Influence.

LATE-STAGE CAREER

Throughout my career, I have met many people who have gotten to the point in their career where they wish to simply do great work without the political headaches that often come with working for larger organizations or being hired through traditional means. Many in this group are seasoned professionals who have had success throughout their careers and have not had occasions to develop a personal network, as they have not needed to do so. As someone who has spent the past twenty-five years working in Chicago, I am quite aware of a couple of Chicago-based companies such as Kraft and Allstate that have prided themselves over the years on developing talent internally and keeping people in their companies for their entire careers.

However, today's business environment is quite different from the business environment many of today's company leaders grew up in. For instance, the average tenure of a CFO in a company today is approximately four to five years. This means most CFOs are moving from company to company (somewhat like a consultant) more often than in the past, and therefore need connections to make things happen and move onto great opportunities.[24]

In order to be successful in identifying opportunities to add value, one needs to know people who will pay for services, whether in the form of a permanent role or an interim consulting role. Therefore, many senior professionals in today's marketplace are attempting to be successful in networking, and those who are most successful approach this from a

---

24 "Age and Tenure in the C Suite," Korn Ferry, Accessed January 23, 2021.

micro-networking perspective and build real relationships. Interestingly, as I have spoken with senior-level professionals over the years, they are often amazed by the fact they already have all the relationships necessary to be wildly successful in building new, sincere relationships. After all, they have worked with and gotten to know many people throughout their lives. They just need to unlock the value in these relationships!

However, most of these people have not proactively maintained or built new relationships by connecting dots from older relationships. Dorie Clark, author of *Reinventing You: Define Your Brand, Imagine Your Future*, agrees with this. "For most professionals, the job offers they receive, and consulting offers they land are a direct result of their network," she says. "If you're not staying in touch with people from your past, you're cutting off a lot of potential opportunities." This creates a unique opportunity to people who are maintaining these relationships and continuing to give into them selflessly.[25]

Most of these more advanced career folks are looking to identify one or two additional opportunities in their career before they retire. The work itself and who they are working with is more important than the company name. However, how does one at this later career stage take proactive steps that help them to identify great, sincere relationships as quickly as possible in order to identify great opportunities? Here are a few exciting ideas to consider:

---

25   Rebecca Knight, "How to Maintain Your Professional Network Over the Years," *Harvard Business Review*, September 20, 2016.

- All the disciplines of the earlier stages apply to this stage as well. The above steps can be compared to the foundation of a house: if you have not built a solid foundation prior, this needs to be a part of your strategy. It needs to be done in parallel with looking for opportunities.
- Identify, today, professional associations specific to your professional area of specialty. Get involved today and attend meetings (virtual or in person). When attending meetings, proactively meet people and follow up by phone and e-mail (LinkedIn messages are fine but try to move communications off LinkedIn as quickly as possible). As mentioned above, join committees, become a leader, and differentiate yourself from others in the organization.
- Create introductions for others, proactively let them know of your desire to meet others and create introductions for them. Share your story of why proactive micro-networking is so important and how it has helped you and others.
- Make these introductions personal. Avoid sending LinkedIn InMail messages as introductions, as it is an impersonal approach. Make this as personal as possible and realize you are building a relationship. Be complimentary when sending these introductions. The more sincerely complimentary you are, the more people will want to reciprocate and help you.
- Do not be afraid to ask for introductions, but realize *you have to give first*. If you do not give first, you have not given someone a reason to give to you.

There are certain things that are common for people at all different times in their lives and careers, and there are a few things that should be thought about at different steps in one's career.

The most important thing to consider is that sincere relationships often do not happen by chance. Of course, there are exceptions. However, where more relationships used to start by chance at the water cooler or in the coffee room at work, given the post-COVID-19 world we are living in, more and more people are working remotely. It is more important to be intentional about creating sincere relationships with those we work with. Given that more and more business is being sold and delivered through online channels, building these sincere relationships will only be more important in the future.

Through living this way and creating sincere relationships for others while creating and maintaining sincere relationships for yourself, will lead to amazing things, including the type of freedom in your life many only dream about.

CHAPTER 7

How Do Companies and Other Entities Create Sincere Business Models That Thrive?

———

"Pay It Forward"

"Be a Giver"

"Make Sure to Network"

These are words we have all heard over and over. In many ways, these expressions have lost their meaning—if they ever had a meaning in the first place. As I have thought about the material for this book and what "sincerity" truly means in its purest form, I continually find myself coming back to these words. I truly believe these are things people want to accomplish—however, I do not believe they know how to do so. Many people believe they are "paying it forward" and "being a Giver," but are we really living this way?

HOW DO LEADERS ACCOMPLISH BEING A GIVER AND BEING SUCCESSFUL

I believe being a Giver means you purely think of others before you think of yourself. Again, it is not something you can fake, and when you are dealing with a real and pure Giver, you tend to know it.

I have a friend who is a top-level senior executive of a global company. When COVID-19 struck, every business in the world was impacted. Employees were unable to go into offices and work physically with coworkers and customers. It was very important to my friend to ensure her teams around the world knew they and their family's health mattered.

She and the rest of her senior management team made sure to intentionally let their teams know how important they and their families were. She explained, "When the new variants began to take place with the virus in Europe, I had worldwide teams working on projects, and some of these people were dealing with sick family members and things like that—literally life and death stuff. Our team and I made sure to let these people personally know they were important and offered any assistance we could provide. It made a huge difference and was just the right thing to do."

This is a great example of a company "walking the walk" rather than just "talking the talk." Employees, and people in general, want to feel taken care of, and my friend and her team didn't just say they cared—they showed it. This is the same thing that should take place in the new relationships you develop as you move through your life.

As I first considered writing a book, I thought the book would be about "networking." As I dug into the stories I included, as well as my own journey, I realized how overused and under-defined this word really was. Most people network to accomplish a short-term outcome—a job, a business transaction, etc. These people will keep relationships to themselves, thinking if they create introductions and opportunities for others, they might lose out on an opportunity for themselves. They come into every conversation looking to "get" rather than "give." They are transactional. But what happens to those who do the complete opposite?

What happens to those who come into these relationships expecting absolutely nothing other than wanting to purely help? Is this a formula for long-term success? These are the real Givers, but how can you live this life successfully? Are companies that foster a sincere and giving culture more successful?

Early in my career, I worked for a well-known staffing/recruiting firm. While there, I met many senior executives of companies large and small. As discussed earlier in the book, my job was to work with these executives, as they had interim or permanent openings on their teams, in partnering to identify the talent to fill these roles. There are various ways of hiring. Companies often use their own internal recruiters to fill permanent roles and will sometimes reach to outside recruitment firms for assistance in filling higher-level or more specialist types of roles. At the same time, as people leave companies, there are often interim needs, and our role was to fill higher-level interim roles quickly to ensure work continued. At times, this included providing talent to assist our clients utilizing a pre-planned schedule, as I described with my friend Lou Fernandez in Chapter Two.

In contrast, at Accenture, our job was to bring in project teams from our firm to implement new technology and processes to make our clients better and more efficient. All of this work was done by people who did not work directly for their client—much like the people I was providing. Consulting firms tend to present themselves as higher-level and able to help their clients to transform their businesses, where staffing firms are there to fill roles.

Rather than selling staffing as staffing firms typically do, from the beginning, I approached it as a consultant looking to understand not just the skillset the client required, but what they were trying to accomplish from a business perspective. This approach set me apart. It also allowed me to differentiate the business model I was representing and to present it in a more sincere way.

Unlike some firms, I was able to recruit and get to know the talent, as well as "sell" the "job order." In this way, I was truly the connector. As I said, the environment was a complete sales environment, bordering on a "boiler room." However, I would naturally get to know both candidates and clients quite well, personally and professionally. I sincerely wanted to get them where they wanted to be, and relationships flourished amazingly as a result!

The business model of these types of recruiting and staffing firms is dependent upon placing talent in companies. If these companies identify this talent without you, you do not get paid. Therefore, there is a built-in incentive to keep relationships to yourself. This often inhibits the ability to develop sincere relationships.

LOOK TO PROVIDE VALUE IN EVERY INTERACTION

Real Givers don't worry about how they will monetize their new relationships; rather, they take the time to understand what "value" means to others. They always look to provide it, and "value" is not always monetary.

From the beginning of my "professional career," I was always the same type of connector I learned to be from my father early in my life and career. The typical selling, selfish behaviors around me simply felt unnatural to me. It was not like me to keep relationships to myself because if I made a sincere introduction, I might not get paid. I understood the model, but I didn't necessarily like it.

From the beginning, I looked to find a balance between being a Giver and ensuring I was not putting my business at risk. If there was ever a doubt, I always did what was in the best interest of the other party rather than putting today's transaction and money first.

As my network of executives grew, people would contact me when they were in transition between roles, looking for my assistance. They realized I had a large and growing rolodex, and they wanted my assistance in meeting people. From the beginning, I would always meet with these people and genuinely look to introduce them to people they would enjoy knowing and who might be helpful to them now or in the future. The more of these sincere introductions you create for others, the deeper and more sincere your relationships will become.

Those who I worked with would ask me, "Why are you making these introductions? If this person lands a role without your help, you will not get paid."

My answer was always the same—"I hope they land a role without my assistance," and further, "I hope someone to whom I introduce them without getting paid helps them land a great job, as that will deepen my relationship with them, make the relationship more real, and will ultimately lead to more trust." From there, it is always easier to do business. Many years later, there are many people I met during these years who I selflessly helped, which led to amazing relationships and to business later in my career. Interestingly, when it came time to discuss business, it was much easier to engage for both sides as trust was already there!

I have realized the fundamental flaw in the thinking of many I have worked with over the years is, they are in too much of a hurry to monetize relationships—and I have found this is how most people and companies think. When I first started in recruiting, relationships mattered. There were no websites such as LinkedIn, Indeed, CareerBuilder, etc. Recruiters actually had to work for a living and get to know the people they were placing, and clients expected the recruiter to know more than just what was on the resume.

Today, anyone with a LinkedIn or CareerBuilder login has access to the same proprietary database I had access to back in the day. The difference is that database was not public. Therefore, recruiters have become lazy and tend to lean on public databases such as LinkedIn and CareerBuilder to identify talent. This is impersonal and does not lead to real relationships.

Recruiters and others who keep relationships to themselves until they can get paid to share them are telling people their ultimate goal is to make money rather than to help. Sincere, long-term relationships are not built in this way. People with this mind-set come into relationships with the number one goal of turning relationships into money-making transactions today. However, the fact is the chances of that happening are very small. The model still being used by many staffing firms is a transactional one, and like the other behaviors I have mentioned, the typical approach to the staffing business. I was able to be successful by coming into relationships with the goal of *giving* without looking for a return. Approaching things transactionally gives you a small chance of creating a business transaction. However, when you treat your employees and clients in the same ways you treat friends, you have a 100 percent chance of building goodwill with those you meet and get to know. This can only lead to great things in the future.

SUCCESS AND FULFILLMENT
THROUGH PURE RELATIONSHIPS

A few years ago, I was introduced to a young man who needed resume assistance. He and I got together and discussed his resume, his career, and what he was looking to achieve both personally as well as professionally. I gave him some very honest feedback and advice. Later on, I introduced him to a couple of people I believed could assist him without looking for anything in return. I sincerely enjoyed doing this.

Many people wonder why I enjoy this so much.

When I came home from college on "double secret probation" after my first semester of my freshman year, my dad had me meet with his accountant, a very successful man with a large firm in downtown Chicago. My father had developed a good friendship with him, and he had offered to meet with me to give me some career advice. After putting on my best suit and heading downtown, I walked into one of the nicest office buildings in the city for the meeting. I sat down in his office and we proceeded to have a very direct conversation about what I had done (and not done) in college, what it took to be successful, and what I would need to do to get there. I realized two things in that meeting. The first thing was I wanted to be successful; the second was I eventually wanted to help others be successful as well. My father's accountant explained to me that although he had been tremendously successfully, at that point in his life, he found true fulfillment in meeting with young people like me and giving them honest advice. This always stuck with me and was something I always tried to do for others as I progressed further in my career.

After giving this young man this very honest and direct feedback, he introduced me to a very high-level senior executive at a large company in Chicago, describing him as brilliant and even more direct than me. I was looking forward to meeting him.

My new relationship invited me for a half hour coffee to get to know one another and talk shop a bit. After an hour and a half, we were still talking about business, family, and life before I needed to leave to a next meeting. I introduced him to a couple of people, he did the same, and we kept in touch over the next few months. I introduced him to a couple of other great people.

A couple of months later, he called me, telling me he and his team needed assistance with a very important project, and he would like to consider my firm. Interestingly, he shared that while he was impressed with my firm, it was the way we met and the fact I did not come into the relationship looking to sell anything that made him more seriously interested in working with my team.

Prior to awarding us the work, he shared with me this was a project that had to be done right because his job was somewhat dependent on the success. He was trusting me personally, as well as our firm, to ensure it went off without a hitch. Even though his boss had never heard of the firm I was with at the time, given how we met and the relationship we were building, he was willing to trust my firm would make him look good since he trusted me. This was a project we had to get right, and it could not have gone better.

This is a perfect example of meeting someone through a business relationship who immediately took on a more personal flavor. Through looking to give first and having something of value to share, we were able to create a relationship that was mutually beneficial. We are good friends to this day!

After this project, he and I discussed why he responded to me and our relationship the way he did. Like anyone at his level, he has dealt with plenty of people trying to sell him services.

"They are mostly full of shit," he said. "They say everything you want to hear, but at the end of the day, they typically just don't deliver."

If I had come into this relationship like most others would, the first meeting I had with him would have been the last. Instead, he was *inspired* to write one of the most glowing introductory e-mails I have ever received, describing me as "someone who cares more about other people than most anyone he has met in business." To this day, our relationship continues to evolve, and we will always take care of one another.

This does not only apply in business, but spans into different areas of life as well.

I am a huge music fan and always have been. Specifically, I am a Deadhead.

I love anything having to do with the Grateful Dead—the music, the culture, the people, everything. I started going to concerts with my best friends in the late 1980s and ended up seeing dozens of shows before Jerry Garcia died in 1995. I still see at least a couple hundred live music events per year.

The first time I ever heard the Grateful Dead was a live tape. It was raw sounding, and my friend who played it for me explained it was a bootleg recording made by a taper of a live show. He further explained the band not only allowed this practic but encouraged it. They sincerely wanted to make music and share it with their fans.

As I have thought more about my experiences in life and business, as well as my reasons for writing this book about sincerity, I wondered if the way I live my personal and professional life has also influenced the music I have been drawn to throughout my life and the culture of the bands I still enjoy to this day.

I was naturally drawn to the freeform nature of the Grateful Dead. I was drawn just as much to the culture of the Deadheads I was meeting at shows and in the parking lot before and after shows, and the relationships I observed between them. They were uniquely genuine and kind. It was an incredibly fun time and was all about people connecting to other human beings in a loving and positive way. It was not just about the music; it was about the shared experience with other human beings—people giving to one another without expecting anything in return.

This was what the culture was all about: sincerity, giving, kindness, and love. It was a band born of the 1960s summer of love. Going to a Grateful Dead concert was not just a musical experience; it was just as much a people experience. But this culture of giving was not just between fans; it was from the band to the fans, and vice versa. From the very beginning, the band allowed their fans to record and trade recordings. They even went so far as to set up a tapers section behind the soundboard and sold specific "taper tickets" for access to this section. These fans would often get early entry to the venue, and the band did not make one dime on these recordings.

Over the years, these tapes began being traded around the country, and as the band toured, more and more people would show up at shows. The Deadhead culture was born. Deadheads would travel the country to see the band and spend time with their friends, meeting new people with whom they shared a common love of music. There was and still is a true sincerity in the culture that simply cannot be faked.

This "accidental business model" ended up being incredibly successful. Through virally sharing the music rather than forcing people to buy the music in order to hear it, they built a huge following around the country. Everywhere they went, they packed arenas, and they ended up one of the most successful rock bands in the history of rock and roll.

"Authorizing tapers and giving them their own section in the crowd never had business-minded rationale," said Dennis McNally, the band's former spokesman and the author of *A Long Strange Trip: The Inside History of the Grateful Dead.* "To stop it would require security measures so draconian that it would ruin the ambience of the show, and the Dead hated being cops."[26]

This accidental, unbelievably successful business model has led other bands to follow the same path. Interestingly, it is the same model through which I have run my life and career, openly sharing relationships with others who can be helpful to them and helping them realize why these relationships are so important.

---

26 Joe Coscarelli, "'Tapers' at the Grateful Dead Concerts Spread the Audio Sacrament," *The New York Times,* July 5, 2015.

Locally in Chicago, the band Mr. Blotto has created an incredible local and national following by employing many of the same principles.

Founded in 1990 by brothers Paul and Mike "Chief" Bolger, Mr. Blotto started out doing Grateful Dead and other blues-related songs in bars around Chicago. From the beginning, they developed a large fan base locally, and they did so not only by playing shows, but by making themselves accessible to their fans in a very unique and sincere way. Ultimately, they simply wanted to have fun making great music for great people.[27] For years they have mounted their own local Lollapalooza-type events called Blottopia and Blottumnal Equinox—and a few years into it, they found themselves with national-type opportunity to take their act to a larger, more national audience.[28]

Much like the Grateful Dead, they encouraged their fans to tape and share the music, trusting they would also buy their albums to support them. Before e-mail, they sent a monthly cartoon card to all fans listing the shows for the month, and they never charged a large cover charge for their shows. I was at many of their early shows and still attend literally hundreds of their shows each year. The sincere relationships I have seen formed due to a common love of this band have changed many people's lives—including mine.

This was not a band that was looking to become a huge national touring act and break the bank. They were looking

27 Mr. Blotto's Website, accessed February 24, 2021.
28 "Blottopia Lineup," Blottopia, accessed February 24, 2021.

to make a living as musicians doing what they loved for a network of fans they loved and who came to love them. By controlling things and managing their career themselves rather than selling out to a record label, they have developed a much more loyal fan base and have not turned into the "machine" other bands often turn into. Many of us have been fans since the beginning. When I go to shows, I see the same faces I have seen for thirty or so years.

The entertainment industry felt the sting of COVID-19 possibly more than any other industry, other than perhaps airlines, hotels and restaurants. Mr. Blotto developed their fan base through live performances; however, thankfully, they had already begun to look at online means of delivering music. They already had an amazingly loyal following, and the fans simply followed them online. They immediately changed their weekly residency show to an online show with an ability to tip the band via Venmo or PayPal. This allowed them to continue reaching their fans across the country with their music.

As I have gone through the personal journey of writing this book, I realized there is very little about my life that has not been impacted by the concept of living the sincerest life I could, surrounded by the sincerest people I could find. I have unknowingly been attracted to cultures and people who are naturally giving. And as I have gotten older, I have seen more and more of the advantages and beauty that this has created in my life and the lives around me.

The Grateful Dead, Mr. Blotto, and many other bands have proven by using an "accidental business model" built on a foundation of giving the music away, much like the careers of professionals who in large part have based their careers on openly sharing relationships and ideas, they can create an unbelievable level of sustainable success through sticking together and sharing with one another.

People who bring the same behaviors to their professional lives these bands accidentally employed are those who will be the most successful going forward. These people never need to look for a job or opportunity, as they can simply rely on their network of sincere relationships. Much like bands that have a loyal fan base, we all need to build our own network of fans. We can accomplish this through taking great care of everyone we meet!

Much like people, companies, and other professional entities that create sincere relationships with their employees, fans, and customers are simply more successful in the long run. However, in order to do this, the lessons learned from The Grateful Dead, Mr. Blotto, and the others about whom I have written are a few examples of what needs to be done. Company leaders need to take a sincere interest in their people as people, not just a collection of skill sets. We need to let our employees know we sincerely care, ask what they want to accomplish, and help them accomplish these things. If we behave sincerely, we will be taken exactly as we intend.

CHAPTER 8

How Can Living a Sincere Lifestyle Lead to Personal and Professional Freedom?

———

New York is one of my favorite cities in the entire world.

As someone who grew up acting and truly wanted to be on Broadway, there is something about New York that is just completely amazing to me. My favorite part of the city is without a doubt the amazing theatrical experiences at your fingertips.

In early 2020, there was talk of a new virus, but no one in the United States was paying much attention. It was early March and my oldest son and I met in New York for a few days of theater and amazing food. In five days, we saw seven shows and had an amazing time!

This was before people realized COVID-19 was a global pandemic. However, there were clear signs that things were moving in that direction. We came home on March 7 and Broadway literally shut down five days later. Life as we all knew it was no longer the same. Relationships have always been important, but there has never been a time in my life where it was so apparent those who had taken a long-term view on relationships were definitely ahead. I shared with my entire network I was writing a book about sincere relationships, and it made for some awesome conversations. It also completely confirmed the thesis of this book—people with sincere, authentic, and intimate relationships are more equipped for success.

On October 14, 2020, the entire world was shut down because of this global pandemic, and Jamie Drake was at Mount Rushmore with her children, living in an amazing camper. Her children were in virtual school (as was a good part of our country) and Jamie was enjoying running her virtual assistant business and the amazing freedom that came with the path she has taken personally and professionally.

How does one achieve this type of freedom? How does one deal with the changes in the marketplace, inevitable economic downturns, and other things that affect our lives personally and professionally, and still come out on top over time?

In the pandemic, the unemployment rate skyrocketed virtually overnight as it significantly impacted many industries. This prompted many people to realize they needed to network but were late to the party and therefore behind the eight ball, as it needs to happen much earlier. Jamie is an outstanding example of someone who has lived her life in such a way it allowed her to thrive in any situation and enjoy incredible freedom at the same time. She is a perfect example of someone who has lived this life from the beginning!

Jamie grew up in the Chicago area and was always a people person. Throughout her childhood, she was a natural performer, always looking for a stage.

She was taught very early on as an actor to be true to herself and those around her, and to be willing to "go there" in relationships with other people. This makes actors great. Many people are quite closed off when they meet new people; however, Jamie is far from closed off. She is naturally warm, engaging, and loves getting to know new people. Jamie went to Harand Camp of the Theatre Arts during the summer when she was a child, and was taught to develop true and sincere relationships with people that would stand the test of time. I went to the same camp for over ten years and learned the same lessons. We all keep in touch with one another forty years later!

Jamie went to college for American Sign Language, which was something that fascinated her, and she became a virtual expert in the language. The only way to learn a language is to immerse yourself with people who are speaking this language. However, Jamie found this to be more difficult at first than immersing herself with people who might speak any other language because of one thing: she was not deaf. During college, she became an interpreter by accident, as people who trusted her would ask her to accompany them to doctor's appointments or personal meetings with attorneys solely because of the trust Jamie had developed in that community.

"The deaf community is incredibly tight-knit," explained Jamie. "In order to really be trusted you need to show up, sincerely and consistently and, just like in any other situation, build real relationships."

In order to accomplish these relationships, Jamie would network in the deaf community. As Jamie tells it, it was her first real taste of networking, and she sincerely enjoyed it and the relationships she built.

"The way I would conduct myself at the bar that hosted Friday Night Deaf Professionals Night was very important to how I built my network in the deaf community, and it led to many of the relationships I still have today," explained Jamie.

The reason for building these relationships was never about getting interpreting gigs; the "why" was sincere, two human beings getting to know one another and developing a natural and organic friendship.

These friendships naturally led to additional interpreting gigs, a business as an American Sign Language interpreter, and showed Jamie the power of developing mutually beneficial relationships.

"My personality and quality of the relationships I was building were far more important than my skill set. I am sure there were better sign language interpreters, but people worked with me due to the trusting relationship we would build with one another."

As Jamie's life began to evolve and she had children, she thought about how she could still run her career, be there for her children, and take great care of these relationships she had developed.

As a single mom, Jamie was someone who not only needed to support her family, but also needed to be there for her children. The prospect of running around the city every day to—often last-minute—interpreting gigs was simply untenable. However, Jamie still had these unbelievable relationships.

On the personal side of her life, Jamie had developed processes to run her business and her personal finances, and as she talked with her network, she realized there were people who needed the services of a virtual assistant. In today's increasingly virtual world, we do not need to show up to an office every day to do our job, and we do not need an assistant who is physically in our same location, which opened up a world of opportunities for Jamie for two reasons:

1. She had a network of sincere relationships that would talk with her about the services she offered and introduce her to others.
2. She had differentiated skills to make a difference in people's lives in these areas.

Jamie now trains other virtual assistants to start their own businesses. She believes strongly in giving value before you ever expect to get business, and she is fine with giving value for free and never getting business. If you look at her website, you will see many examples of ideas Jamie gives away for free. I wondered, why would Jamie be willing to do this? Why would she give advice for free that others were out in the marketplace simply trying to sell?

"I believe in giving value before ever expecting anything," said Jamie. "I am confident that through selflessly giving value and building real relationships with people, opportunities will emerge, and this is exactly what has taken place in my life and my business." Jamie agrees these relationships fit the definition of 360-degree, multi-dimensional relationships perfectly!

No one could ever forecast the type of market downturns that took place in 2000 and 2008, or the global pandemic that took place in 2020. Those who have set up their lives in the way Jamie has are best able to withstand these times, as they can turn to their sincere relationships for real and sincere support.

Jamie always had a goal of attaining the most freedom she could. By running a virtual assistant business and teaching others to work virtually, Jamie could literally work from anywhere.

Therefore, when it became clear in 2020 her children would go to school virtually, it was a perfect opportunity to make lemonade from lemons. She bought an RV and headed out on the road with her two daughters to spend time together and see the country. Each morning, she handled her business responsibilities while her kids were in virtual school, and after, they had true freedom to explore national parks and other amazing places they were never able to visit together.

The lesson here is the more sincere and real relationships we build throughout our lives, and the more we break down the walls between our personal and professional relationships, the more successful and fulfilled we will all be. Jamie did these things throughout her entire life, and when the chips were down, she was much more prepared to weather the storm!

Allan Loeb is another example of someone whose ability to build and maintain sincere relationships has led to amazing success in one of the most difficult and cutthroat of industries: entertainment.

If there is any place with less of a chance of finding success, it is probably Hollywood, yet every year, young, starry-eyed folks from around the country head to Hollywood, California, with a dream of making it big—actors, actresses, screenwriters, directors, etc. They all have the same goal, and they are competing for only a handful of jobs.

Allan Loeb was but one of these folks in the early 1990s. After completing his undergraduate degree in New York, unsure what he wanted to do after school, Allan did what many young people do—asked his family to help him get a job. His father had some connections at the Chicago Board of Trade, and he scored a job as a runner. This meant his job was to be on the trading floor, which back in the day was a loud, bustling pit of men yelling at one another to trade currencies. He hated it.

"That was a job," he said. "I didn't love it. At the same time, a friend of mine was writing screenplays in Hollywood, and I took an interest in his scripts and started giving him notes.

That led me down the rabbit hole. I took a class, I was hooked, and I found myself living in California."

After a bit of time, he had some minor success. In 1997, he sold his first script to DreamWorks, a romantic comedy titled *The Second Time Around*. In 1998, he was successful in selling a baseball dramedy called *The 7th Game* to United Artists. In May 2001, he sold his spec thriller *Protection* to Davis Entertainment and 20th Century Fox. While this was his third script sold as a writer, it did not give him the income necessary to live his life. During this entire time in Hollywood, Allan did what he had always done—he got to know people around town and built sincere friendships and relationships. He did not realize how important those relationships would be in the future. When I say he was fun to be around, I should know. He is one of my greatest and longest friends.[29]

Allan also had a secret. He was a severe gambling addict. Some weekends, he would lose up to thirty thousand dollars, and by 2004, he found himself one hundred fifty thousand dollars in credit card debt.

"I am moving to New York as I need to get out of Los Angeles and away from the behaviors I have become addicted to. I am going to move to New York, where my *Hail Mary* script will be set," he said. This became the movie with Pierce Brosnan and Kate Beckinsale that was released in 2017 called *The Only Living Boy in New York*.

---

29   Allan Loeb IMDB Page, accessed February 24, 2021.

"Gambling was a time suck, an energy suck, a creativity suck. I started going to Gamblers Anonymous meetings every Thursday night in New York, and the writing flourished. It had so much more energy and passion."[30]

Allan's gambling addiction had truly become the major focus of his life, and thankfully, he had an amazing group of real friends who had his back through that entire time. I am proud to have been one of them.

Allan is undoubtedly talented, but there are many talented people in Hollywood. Each year, thousands of people head to Hollywood looking for stardom, but only a handful are successful. Talent is table stakes in Hollywood, and plenty of people simply have little. "But those who foster relationships around town are always the most sustainably successful," explained Loeb, and this was something he did extremely well. Sincerity and sincere relationships can drive sustainability in your life!

To prove his talent, Allan had not one, but two scripts end up in the top four spots on the inaugural 2005 Black List of Best Unproduced Scripts in Hollywood, as identified by agents, directors, producers, and other industry folks.

After spending a few months in New York writing the script for *The Only Living Boy in New York* and attending Gamblers Anonymous meetings, he got the news he had been waiting for his entire career. It was the moment when his life would completely change.

---

30   Jay A. Fernandez, "Former Gambler Now in the Chips," *Chicago Tribune*, September 7, 2006.

"Literally the day I wrote "Fade In" on my script, I got a call from my agent in Los Angeles that DreamWorks wanted to make *Things We Lost in the Fire* with Benicio del Toro, Halle Berry, and David Duchovny," Allan explained. The movie would have to be fast-tracked, meaning it would move through the process to get to the screen quickly. This was one of the movies that had made the Black List—the other was *The Only Living Boy in New York*.[31]

Since the success of *Things We Lost in the Fire,* Allan has almost literally not stopped typing. Given he spent over twenty years building relationships with folks around town, he is likable and talented; he has stayed extremely busy.

As Allan said, it isn't usually the most talented people who are successful in Hollywood; rather, it is those who stick to it, develop relationships, and are loyal. There really are not a ton of sincere behaviors in Hollywood, and as was discussed earlier in the Mario Armstrong story, it is those who build and maintain authentic and sincere relationships over time who are usually most successful and fulfilled.

But what specifically did Allan do during those years? What can we learn from what Allan did that might help you develop the relationships you need to make your life and career better and more fulfilled?

Like Mario, Allan has mentored many people in his industry, and many of these people have gone on to amazing success and become household names. The advice he gives these folks

---

31   Ibid.

is much the same advice he has followed over the past twenty-five years of meeting people and building the relationships that have been necessary for him to be successful.

Most people tend to approach a networking meeting as a meeting rather than the beginning of a relationship. Allan suggests we use these initial meetings as the beginning of a relationship. Just like in other industries, those who are most successful in Hollywood approach every meeting looking to build a mutually beneficial relationship that will be interesting to both sides.

Allan gives very specific advice to young people he meets with in terms of how they should approach meetings, and this advice applies to most any profession at any level. It applies when you are young, but it also applies if you are trying to make any pivot and build any relationship in your life.

This advice can apply to any industry and is a great roadmap to follow to use a first meeting as a starting point to the building of a great, long-term relationship. These are additional practical steps that can be followed immediately and throughout the rest of your life and career to enrich your life!

1. *Remember, you're not just getting advice from these people. There's a chance one of them may give you a job or internship in the future. I hear stories all the time about someone who "gave advice" to a college kid years ago and now they're working together on a huge project or are business partners in a new venture.*
2. *Research who you're talking to and make sure to mention one or two things casually to them that prove you've done your homework. i.e., "Google says you grew up in*

Germany—when did you to move to America?" or "My uncle says you're a huge Sixers fan, do you like the Doc Rivers hire?" Drop shit like that in if you can. It goes a long way.

3. *People want to talk about themselves. This is probably the most important thing you'll ever learn in life. Let them. Questions like "So I was thinking about going to law school but am not sure—do you think I should?" should be rephrased like "Did you go to law school? (if so) Do you think it was beneficial? (if not) Do you regret it?" Change all "I" questions to "you"—the more it's about them, the better it will help you.*

4. *Ask for stories. People love to tell stories about themselves. Literally say, "What's the story with how you ended up representing Dan Levy?" "I appreciate your time so you can tell me the short version, but I really wanna hear the story of how you ended up in Hollywood from Kansas." You will get great advice and teachable moments from their stories, and they will like you more by telling them. Once again, I **cannot** stress this enough...the more they talk about themselves, the more they like you. People don't give a shit about you—they're obsessed with themselves. This is true for everybody (whether they know it or not).*

5. *Tap into passion, not fame, money, or glamour. Good questions to that effect are "What about your profession would you do for free?" "What is the best thing about what you do that has nothing to do with money, power, or success?" "Have you had opportunities to leave your current position for more money but didn't? (if so) Can I hear the story about that?" That will get them talking about what gives their lives meaning. That's the best thing to learn about what makes a career worth pursuing.*

6. *Instead of asking them what you should do, ask them this: "Knowing what you do now, what advice would you give your twenty-year-old self today?" "How is entering your profession different in 2021 than it was when you came into the field?"*

7. *Instead of asking what you need to be doing to get good at something, ask them this: "What qualities, talents, and attributes are most important to do your profession?" Side note—I use the words "profession" and "career," never "job." Nobody wants a job; everybody wants a career.*

8. *Instead of "what books should I read" or "what websites should I check out," ask, What books did you read along the way that helped you become as successful as you are? (People like being told they're successful; there isn't a human this isn't true about.) What podcasts do you listen to? What webpages do you like? What's a good movie or novel that shows your profession in the most realistic light? (Everybody has a favorite work of fiction about their professions—many joined that profession because of that work of fiction!) Here's a bigger tip—go watch that movie or read that book, then e-mail the person and tell them what you loved about it a few weeks later—they will remember you!*

9. *What are the biggest issues currently in your profession that could threaten it or make it more exciting? (Get them talking about the landscape and they'll remember you as being informed—even if you don't say shit.)*

If you approach any new relationship with genuine curiosity, passion, and a sincere desire to learn and add value over time, the quality of the relationships in your life will soar and your life will be that much better, easier, and more fulfilled as a result!

Conclusion

————

What do you do when you are used to being out seeing clients and friends and suddenly the entire world shuts down—**literally**?

This is the situation in which I found myself in March 2020 when the COVID-19 pandemic hit. I ended up leaving the firm I had been with for over eight years, and I was intent on making a pivot toward representing services that were less commoditized and more about helping people *grow* their businesses rather than simply making them more efficient or filling a role with a quality professional.

I found myself extremely busy catching up with people I had met throughout my career. Many people who were not easily available in the past were more easily reachable, as many of the senior executives I know typically traveled extensively. Given all travel was shut down, they had additional time they rarely had.

Given I had built great relationships, people would get back to me and I heard the same thing from many of them. They missed connecting with and seeing people.

Since we could not attend networking events and such, people were looking for ways to connect. As I mentioned in an earlier chapter, I created my own group to connect executives to one another, to become more of a Center of Influence. I jumped online, bought my Zoom account, and set up a weekly call for fifteen of my senior executive-level friends. We discussed topics such as how to network in a virtual environment and how to ensure they were differentiating themselves as they were meeting new people. It was awesome that these folks connected to one another, and I was the reason. It not only deepened every single relationship, but it was also completely sincere.

Relationship building and pursuing your best personal and professional life are about more than just attending networking events; it is about the authentic relationships you develop with those you meet. You do not always have to meet these people in order to find ways to give into the relationship.

Those who approach their professional lives in a transactional way are setting themselves up for the opposite of what they seek! Instead, it is those who develop real, sincere, and organic relationships who enjoy the most long-term success.

What is truly important is becoming a Center of Influence for as many people as you can, truly thinking of helping others over transactions, and being consistent in these behaviors over time.

Most of the people you meet personally or professionally will probably not live their lives this way, and that is your opportunity. It may feel risky to you, and if you are in any way risk-averse, you may be hesitant to follow through with the recommendations I have made. But if you have taken the time to read this book and the amazing examples from extraordinary people, what do you have to lose by giving it a try? Find two people you know well and introduce them through a well-written e-mail. Let them know of the book you have read, and the incredible lives people are living through sincerity. I can virtually guarantee you will stand out from others and your life will become more outstanding and inspiring to others.

Therein lies your opportunity to be different. Aspire to be like my father Clifford Brooks, Loren Michaels Harris, Lou Fernandez, Janet Zelenka, Mario Armstrong, Barry Masek, Paige Arnof-Fenn, Allan Loeb, Benny Mathew, and Jamie Drake. Become a Center of Influence in your community and industry, and always look to sincerely help those around you as selflessly as possible.

I've always known these principles to be true in my own life, but writing this book has only solidified my message as universally true. It isn't a fluke that I've found success and fulfillment through living the "360-degree, multi-dimensional relationship" life. It's just the natural result of implementing these principles in my life. I've seen it played out in the stories of countless others as I've explored these concepts for this book!

As you implement these strategies, you will undoubtedly become more and more comfortable with the work-life integration concept. Take one of your professional relationships—whether it is a peer, client, or boss—and take it in a more personal direction, see what happens. Of course, when doing this, we need to read people a bit; but I have been amazed some of the people who have been most inspired by this approach are those who were most skeptical at first.

Earlier in this book, I mentioned my friend who moved and has created an amazing network of friends and business associates. This only took three years and was done by utilizing many of the concepts and frameworks suggested in this book. When we recently reconnected, he excitedly shared with me that through applying these concepts, he has created an amazing life for himself and his family in a new city. Keep in mind, he was skeptical of the approach, but once he jumped in, the water was fine.

As you move through your career living life this way, or if you are in the middle or later part of your career, you will undoubtedly see the quality of your relationships change, and those you develop relationships with will change as well. As you are exposed to sincerer Givers, your willingness to put up with environments that are filled with Takers professionally will diminish. You will gravitate to business models where sincerity and revenue are both possible. These pure, sincere business models certainly exist and thrive.

Before you know it, your entire life can be different!

Like anything we do in life, it takes a first step. Without the first step, you cannot take the second and third. If you live your life in the ways that are described in this book, you will live an amazing life and help many people along the way. You will accomplish your hopes and dreams, and you will help others do the same. In order to find your greatest success throughout your life, living a sincere life will take you a very long way by accomplishing your personal hopes and dreams and, just as importantly, helping many people along the way.

How could life get better than that?

Acknowledgments

I would like to thank the following people for their amazing support and encouragement of this project and, for that matter, everything I have done in my life and will do going forward.

- My family, for their support every single day of my life—my wife Lisa Brooks, my kids Andrew, Dylan and Leo, and my two awesome Golden Retrievers, Jerry and Scarlet.
- My father, Clifford Brooks, who, as I discussed in the book, taught me everything about relationships in business.
- My mother, Judy Brooks, who is a constant volunteer and is one of the most giving people I know—I learned everything I know about being a Giver from her.
- My in-laws, Diane and David Heller, who have been there to support our family in every way possible. David, unfortunately, passed away, but I know he is proud of this accomplishment. I have him to thank for pushing me to become the best person and professional I could become, and for so much more. My mother-in-law Diane is a rock for our family, someone I appreciate every single day, and one of the most giving people you will ever meet.

- I have too many friends than are possible to list here—I want every single one of them to know the individual relationship I have with them is important and special to me, and without them, I am not sure this project would have been possible.

Furthermore, I would like to thank the individuals who supported my book:

Adam Ortega
Allan Loeb
Andrew Burke
Anna Kooi
Anna Kroner
Ashbey Riley
Barry Metzger
Becky Markovich
Ben Yao
Betty Pigman
Bob Bernstein
Brad Gavelek
Brent Novoselsky
Brian W. Lauer
Brian O'Keane
Bryan Mittelman
Carlo Mahfouz
Carol Okamoto
Cheryl Wittenstein
Chris Burd
Christopher Cotteleer
Christopher Peckham
Chuck LaMantia
Chuck Schweiger

Dan Argentar
Dan Jenks
Dan Kardatzke
Daniel Struck
Darin Aprati
David Schiff
David Waxman
Diane Heller
Daniel K. Gallas
Douglas Berg
Edward Ross
Eric Koester
Eric Levinson
Frances Rush
Frank Cesario
Gail Holmberg
Gary Plaster
Gary Rabishaw
Gregg Mellinger
Gregory Mayer
Gregory J. Silverman
Harry Zander
Jake Paschen
James Burns
James J. McCarthy
James W. Rosenberger
Jan Lofgren
Janet Karabas
Janet Zelenka
Jeff Cohn
Jeff Lubow
Jennifer Jones

Jennifer Turk
Jim Blickendorf
Jim Komar
Jim Marshall
Jill Kirshenbaum
Jill Rhodes
Joel Brown
John Carley
John Saunders
Jonathan Reed
Jonathan Shaw
Katie Gazdacka
Kathy Kilroy
Kevin Glassberg
Kevin Nemetz
Kevin O'Grady
Kristi Ramirez
Ken Glazier
Ken Kushibab
Kimberly Flaherty
Larry Mason
Lauren Russ
Lawrence B. Aaron
Lee Boyce
Lee Leiderman
Leonard Tenner
Lisa Datz
Lisa Schulkin
Lon Blumenthal
Lou Fernandez
Luke A. Heerema
Lynn Yanow

Maggie Martensen
Mark Goldberg
Mark Wyckoff
Martijn van Harten
Martin J. Garvin
Martin Kierzek
Martin Ross
Mary Mulhern
Matthew Behr
Matthew Goodman
Melissa Forman Levin
Melinvermont
Michael Cimarusti
Michael J. Hoffman
Monica Kornberg
Natalie Mashaal
Nicholas Innocenzi
Nick Blawat
Nina Graham
Pam Scheferman
Patrick Barton
Rebecca Masson
Richard Hoffman
Rick Gray
Rick Hans
Rob Johnson
Rob Wilkerson
Robert J. Havey
Robert A. Pagorek
Ronald Gauvin
Sam Santhanam
Sergey Kochergan

Seymour "Skip" Newman

Scott A. Stringer

Scott Forester

Shannon Boyle

Stephen Bowater

Steve Doner

Steven Brown

Steven Ginsburg

Susan Gidley

Ted Belinky

Teresa Krafcisin

Terri Visovatti

Todd Brown

Todd Snyder

Tom Woytych

Yolanda Daniel

Zeljko Kecman

I would also like to thank the group of beta readers who supported my campaign and gave me feedback on my writing, as well as those who allowed their inspiring stories to be told—I sincerely appreciate it:

Lisa Brooks

Andrew Brooks

Clifford Brooks

Allan Loeb

Barry Masek

Benny Mathew

Darin Aprati

Jamie Drake

Janet Zelenka

Jeff Lubow
Kevin Nemetz
Loren Michaels Harris
Lou Fernandez
Mario Armstrong
Nick Blawat
Paige Arnof-Fenn
Rick Gray
Terri Visovatti
Rob Johnson

The boys in Mr. Blotto—Paul Bolger, Mike "Chief" Bolger, Mark Hague, Alan Baster, David Allen, and Steve Ball

Special thanks goes out to: Professor Eric Koester, everyone at the Creator Institute at Georgetown University, and everyone at New Degree Press, with special thanks to Chelsea Friday, Anne Snyder, Brian Bies, and John Saunders.

Appendix

INTRODUCTION

- LinkedIn Corporate Communications. "Eighty-Percent of Professionals Consider Networking Important to Career Success." LinkedIn Pressroom, June 22, 2017. https://news.linkedin.com/2017/6/eighty-percent-of-professionals-consider-networking-important-to-career-success.

- Minor, Lloyd. "Listening is Fundamental: The mystery of sound and how it affects us." *Stanford Medicine,* Spring 2018. https://stanmed.stanford.edu/listening/dean-lloyd-minor-on-importance-listening-hearing-research.html.

CHAPTER 1

- Floyd, Kory, PhD. "What Lack of Affection Can Do to You." *Psychology Today,* August 31, 2013. https://www.psychologytoday.com/us/blog/affectionado/201308/what-lack-affection-can-do-you.

- Northwestern Medicine. "Five Benefits of Healthy Relationships." Accessed February 11, 2021. https://www.nm.org/healthbeat/healthy-tips/5-benefits-of-healthy-relationships.

- *Vocabulary Online,* s.v. "Sincerity." Accessed February 14, 2021. https://www.vocabulary.com/dictionary/sincerity.

CHAPTER 3

- An, Mimi. "How Salespeople Learn." *HubSpot* (blog). December 11, 2019, accessed February 14, 2021. https://blog.hubspot.com/sales/how-salespeople-learn?ga=2.221430040.1405539683.1599855319-242315361.1598664163.

- Grant, Adam. *Give and Take: A Revolutionary Approach to Success.* New York: Penguin Group, 2013.

- Hu, Charlotte. "Demystifying Love: The Science Behind Human Relationships." Dailybreak. June 27, 2017. Accessed February 11, 2021. https://www.dailybreak.com/break/the-science-behind-human-relationships.

- Newman, Kira, Jill Suttie, Jeremy Adam Smith, Emiliana R. Simon-Thomas and Elizabeth Svoboda. "The Top 10 Insights from the "Science of a Meaningful Life" in 2020." *Greater Good Magazine.* December 17, 2020. https://greatergood.berkeley.edu/article/item/the_top_10_insights_from_the_science_of_a_meaningful_life_in_2020.

- *TED.* "Adam Grant: Are You a Giver or a Taker?" January 24, 2017, video, 13:28. https://www.youtube.com/watch?v=YyXRYg-jQXXo.

CHAPTER 4

- *BLS Spotlight on Statistics: The Recession of 2007–2009:* US Bureau of Labor Statistics, February 2012.

- Donovan, Gordon. "9/11: Then and now — 18 years later." *Yahoo! News*, September 10, 2019. https://www.yahoo.com/news/911-then-and-now-18-years-later-182946226.html.

- Segal, Troy. "Enron Scandal: The Fall of a Wall Street Darling." Investopedia, updated January 19th, 2021. https://www.investopedia.com/updates/enron-scandal-summary/.

- Silverman, Rachel. "Accenture Posts 4th-Quarter Loss, Plans Charge Related to Attacks." *Wall Street Journal,* October 12, 2001. https://www.wsj.com/articles/SB1002813286331449560.

- US Bureau of Labor Statistics. "Extended Mass Layoffs and the 9/11 Attacks." Accessed January 23, 2021. https://www.bls.gov/opub/ted/2003/sept/wk2/art03.htm?view_full.

CHAPTER 5

- Cheng-Tozum, Dorcas. "Work-Life Balance vs. Work-Life Integration: How Are They Different and Which One Is For You?" *Inc.com,* March 14, 2018. https://www.inc.com/dorcas-cheng-tozun/how-work-life-integration-can-help-you-have-it-all.html.

- Gregg, Eric. "The Cost of Internal Employee Turnover in Staffing." *Clearly Rated (blog),* December 12, 2019. https://www.clearlyrated.com/solutions/the-cost-of-internal-employee-turnover-in-staffing/.

- Marioarmstrong.com. "Mario Armstrong: Motivating People around the World to Never Settle." Accessed January 30, 2021. https://www.marioarmstrong.com/about-2/marios-bio/.

CHAPTER 6

- Grant, Adam. *Give and Take* New York, Penguin USA: 2013.

- Knight, Rebecca. "How to Maintain Your Professional Network Over the Years." *Harvard Business Review,* September 20, 2016. https://hbr.org/2016/09/how-to-maintain-your-professional-network-over-the-years.

- Korn Ferry. "Age and Tenure in the C Suite." Accessed January 23, 2021. https://www.kornferry.com/about-us/press/age-and-tenure-in-the-c-suite#.

- Sinek, Simon. *Start with Why.* New York: Penguin Publishing Group, 2009.

CHAPTER 7

- Blottopia. "Blottopia Lineup." Accessed February 24, 2021. http://blottopia.com/lineup/.

- Coscarelli, Joe. "'Tapers' at the Grateful Dead Concerts Spread the Audio Sacrament." *The New York Times,* July 5, 2015. https://www.nytimes.com/2015/07/06/arts/music/tapers-at-the-grateful-dead-concerts-spread-the-audio-sacrament.html.

- Mr. Blotto's Website. Accessed February 24, 2021. https://www.mrblotto.net/.

CHAPTER 8

- Allan Loeb's IMDB Page. Accessed February 24, 2021. https://www.imdb.com/name/nm1615610/?ref_=fn_al_nm_1.

- Fernandez, Jay A. "Former Gambler Now in the Chips." *Chicago Tribune*, September 7, 2006. https://www.chicagotribune.com/la-et-scriptland27sep27-story.html.

Made in the USA
Monee, IL
24 May 2021

69406179R00105